YOUR JESUS IS TOO SMALL

YOUR JESUS IS TOO SMALL

The Collapse of Christian Character

Douglas J. Miller

Foreword by Tony Campolo

CASCADE *Books* • Eugene, Oregon

YOUR JESUS IS TOO SMALL
The Collapse of Christian Character

Copyright © 2018 Douglas J. Miller. All rights reserved. Except for brief quotations in critical publications or reviews, no part of this book may be reproduced in any manner without prior written permission from the publisher. Written Permissions, Wipf and Stock Publisher, 199 W. 8th Ave. Suite 3, Eugene, OR 97401.

Cascade Books
An Imprint of Wipf and Stock Publishers
199 W. 8th Ave., Ste. 3
Eugene, OR 97401

www.wipfandstock.com

PAPERBACK ISBN: 978-1-5326-1778-2
HARDCOVER ISBN: 978-1-4982-4274-5
EBOOK ISBN: 978-1-4982-4273-8

Cataloging-in-Publication data:

Names: Miller, Douglas J., author | Campolo, Tony, foreword.

Title: Your Jesus is too small : the collapse of Christian character / Douglas J. Miller ; foreword by Tony Campolo.

Description: Eugene, OR: Cascade Books, 2018 | Includes bibliographical references.

Identifiers: ISBN: 978-1-5326-1778-2 (paperback) | ISBN: 978-1-4982-4274-5 (hardcover) | ISBN: 978-1-4982-4273-8 (ebook).

Subjects: LCSH: Jesus Christ—Significance | Virtue | Discipleship.

Classification: BT102 M55 2018 (paperback) | BT102 (ebook).

Manufactured in the U.S.A.   02/05/18

Unless otherwise noted, Scripture quotations contained herein are from the New Revised Standard Version Bible, copyright © 1989, Division of Christian Education of the National Council of Churches of Christ in the USA.

To Sandra Lynn Miller

My spouse and dearest friend
who lives the exalted Jesus everyday
by her longstanding service as a nurse to students
and by her humble dedication to the most vulnerable
and despised in our society, namely, the houseless

Contents

Foreword by Tony Campolo | ix

Introduction | 1

Part 1: Belittling Jesus | 11

1 A Simply-saving-souls Jesus | 22
2 A Fire-escape Jesus | 27
3 A Pie-in-the-sky Jesus | 33
4 A Prosperity-sugar-daddy Jesus | 37
5 A Sentimental Jesus | 42
6 A Stained-glass Jesus | 46
7 A Doctrinaire Jesus | 50
8 A Legalistic-judgmental Jesus | 54
9 A Positive-thinking Jesus | 59
10 An Anti-intellectual Jesus | 62
11 A Magical-thinking Jesus | 66
12 A Problem-solving Jesus | 72
13 A Quick-fix Jesus | 75
14 An Intolerant Jesus | 81
15 An End-times Jesus | 87
16 A Flag-waving-warrior Jesus | 91
17 A Subdue-our-Earth Jesus | 95
18 A Wing-nut Jesus | 98

Part 2: Exalting Jesus | 103

19 The Galilean-peasant Jesus | 107

20 The Jewish–prophet Jesus | 111

21 The Divine-sovereign Jesus | 114

22 The Neighbor-serving Jesus | 117

23 The Compassionate Jesus | 120

24 The Justice-minded Jesus | 125

25 The Welcoming Jesus | 130

26 The Spirit-of-the-law Jesus | 136

27 The Non-materialist Jesus | 140

28 The Forgiving Jesus | 144

29 The Truth-seeking Jesus | 148

30 The Peace-loving Jesus | 153

31 The Union-of-nations Jesus | 158

32 The Creation-care Jesus | 161

33 The Progressive Jesus | 165

34 The Character-transforming Jesus | 169

35 Conclusion | 172

Bibliography | 175

Foreword

George Bernard Shaw once said, "God created man in His image and then man returned the favor."

What Shaw declared is all too evident in American Christianity. We have replaced the Jesus who is revealed in the Gospels, who was and is an incarnation of God, with an American Jesus who is an embodiment of who we are and an incarnation of our values.

In a more sophisticated and expanded form, this same idea was expounded by Emil Durkheim more than a century ago, in his book, *The Elementary Forms of the Religious Life*. Durkheim pointed out that each societal system tends to create a deity which embodies its most positive traits, characteristics and values, and then worships that deity, not realizing that in so doing they are really worshiping themselves.

The Apostle Paul picks up the same theme in Romans chapter 1 when he writes that people take the incorruptible God and transform this God into an image likened unto corruptible humanity.

In this book, Doug Miller does the work of a prophet who comes with a sledgehammer to smash the false idols that we have constructed in place of the biblical Jesus. With the insights of an academic, but in the language of a typical layperson, he deconstructs the American Jesus in order to clear the way for us to encounter the true historical Jesus as revealed in Scripture.

As I travel across America and listen to sermons from pulpits, and take in what I all too often hear described from an array of television evangelists, along with a host of radio Bible teachers, is a Jesus who comes across as a white Anglo-Saxon Protestant, rather than the transcendent God of Scripture. What's even worse is that Jesus is being politicized. I find that Christian Republicans try to make Jesus into a purveyor of their Conservative politics and they search through Scripture to find verses that will legitimate their laissez faire economics and their hyper American individualism. On the other hand, I travel with a lot of religious Democrats who try to make Jesus into an archetype of their political ideology.

Any thinking person will realize that the Jesus we find in the gospels is neither a Democrat nor a Republican, but instead transcends political ideologies and comes with judgment on the platforms of each of the major political parties of America. To mix the biblical Jesus with politics of either party is like mixing ice cream with horse manure. Ice cream will not hurt the manure, but the manure will surely have a distasteful effect on the ice cream.

The American-created Jesus, unlike the biblical Jesus, promises to deliver the good life that is propagated in the concept of the American Dream. He promises economic prosperity to the faithful and gives us a belief in ourselves that will enable us to be successful in all of life's ventures. He is a Jesus that promises success competitively achieved and calls his followers to embrace American rugged individualism and, when necessary, American militarism. As our soldiers go off to war in a place like Iraq, our cultural religion leads us to assume that Jesus is on their side for the very simple reason that we have made him into one of them. He's an American!

Prayer to this American deity contradicts the definitions of religion of sociologists such as Bronislaw Malinoski, and better fit his definition of magic. Magic, he says, is an appeal to higher powers to do *our* will, whereas true religion leads to us surrendering to the higher powers to do their will. Too much of American religion reeks of magic.

The Jesus that I find propagated far too often in our society has, as his primary mission, to get people into Heaven when they die; whereas, as we find in the initial words of Christ in each of the three synoptic Gospels, his main mission was and is to declare that "The Kingdom of God is at hand." The biblical Jesus makes it clear to his disciples that his Kingdom is something that he wants to see happen here on earth, and he asks them to pray for that Kingdom to come in this world when he taught them to pray The Lord's Prayer. Insights into the nature of that Kingdom are found in all of his parables.

The Jesus of Scripture is not so much committed to otherworldliness as he is committed to changing this world into the kind of world that he wills for it to be. That Kingdom is a society in which all institutions are transformed into models of justice, and the people who live in that society are, themselves, transformed into having Christ-like characteristics.

Foreword

It seems to me that mainline denominations have done a good job talking about social transformation in this world, but have not paid enough attention to individualistic salvation for the afterlife; whereas "cultural Christians" have done the reverse. Obviously, we need both. The holistic Gospel we find in the message of Jesus requires that we not only be concerned about social change, but also personal change, which is the work that the Holy Spirit does in our lives.

Over the last few years, a new movement has arisen, primarily among young people, called Red Letter Christians (see www.redletterchristians.org). To date, as many as five million people around the globe have logged onto the website of this movement, being hungry for the Jesus who is revealed in those red letters found in many Bibles. I think most of us can recall seeing such Bibles in which the words of Jesus are highlighted in red. That Red Letter Jesus is the Jesus that Doug Miller endeavors to bring to us in this book.

One of the leaders of this Red Letter Christians movement is Shane Claiborne, a popular speaker and author among those who are in the upcoming generation of millennials. As a keynote speaker for the National Youth Convention a few years ago, Shane did something that stunned his audience. He took to the pulpit and announced, "You are about to hear the greatest sermon ever preached!!!"

Needless to say, people were shocked at his brashness. The idea that this young man was about to preach the *greatest* sermon ever preached seemed like the epitome of arrogance. But Shane defused that concern when he opened the Bible and read chapters 5, 6, and 7 of Matthew (The Sermon on the Mount). When he finished, Shane closed the Bible and then said, "We'll all agree, won't we, that that is the greatest sermon ever preached." He paused and said, "But we're not going to take Jesus seriously. We think he was only kidding." He then sat down.

Shane hit all of his listeners, including myself, in a very vulnerable spot. He asked the question that needs to be asked, the question we would like to avoid, "Are we going to take the Jesus as we find him speaking to us in the red letters of the Bible seriously, and are we going to commit to do what he asks us to do?" Or are we going to worship the Americanized version of Jesus that the author of this book endeavors to deconstruct?

Gandhi once said that everyone in the world knows what Jesus taught in The Sermon on the Mount—except for Christians. That is a horrendous indictment, but it is true. How many of us are ready to do what Jesus told

Foreword

us to do with our money, as outlined in The Sermon on the Mount or in his proposal to the rich young ruler as recorded in Mark 10? Gandhi also asked the simple question as to whether anyone can read The Sermon on the Mount and not come away convinced that Jesus advocated nonviolent resistance to evil, and especially to war.

To those who say Christian ethics are not as simple as all of that, I ask them to remember Mark Twain's comment, "Most people are bothered by those passages of Scripture they do not understand, but the passages that bother me are those I do understand." Those passages trouble me, too.

When Jesus calls us to be his disciples, according to Dietrich Bonhoeffer, he bids us to come and die. This implies that we set aside the consumeristic ventures of our everyday lives in order to seek first the Kingdom of God and his righteousness (i.e., justice). This is hard to do, and that's why we are tempted to replace the biblical Jesus with our made-up one. In 2 Corinthians 11:4, Paul writes that there will come those who will deliver another Christ than the one who came to save us. I think that far too often American Christianity has been seduced into presenting another Jesus than the one who came to seek and save us from our distorted concepts of what it means to be His followers. Doug Miller, in this book, is attempting to help us to get back to the true Jesus—*the biblical One*, as expressed in those red letters of Scripture.

Tony Campolo, PhD
Eastern University

Introduction

We can make Jesus look quite small if we are not careful. This book explores how we unwittingly belittle him in the face of his awe-inspiring grandeur. Over fifty years ago, J. B. Phillips, the Anglican priest whose paraphrase of the New Testament bears his name, wrote an eye-opening little book with a big message titled *Your God Is Too Small*. Phillips lamented that many "have not found a God big enough for modern needs."[1] Phillips wanted us to enlarge our "unintelligent, naïve, or immature" concepts of God, mostly inherited from childhood. He encouraged Christians to dispel their "Unreal Gods" like the "Residential Policeman" (a tyrant God), the "Grand Old Man" (an old-fashioned God), "the God-in-a-Box" (a church-confined God), and a dozen other common misconceptions. He decried that something so grand, sublime, and elevated, could be made so tiny, trivial, and debased, inhibiting us from "catching a glimpse of the true God."[2] Inevitably, when Christians belittle God, they also belittle Jesus.

For Phillips, these degraded concepts of God contribute to a "decline in our moral sense" and a "morbidly developed conscience" that we "wrongly consider to be the voice of God."[3] Fifty years later, the questions still loom: have we Christians progressed in magnifying God since Phillips's warnings or, sadly, have we actually made God even smaller? Does God today command less admiration and respect? Has our moral sense shriveled even further, given we live in a "post-truth" world where lies are trumped up and deceit is normalized? Has something horrible befallen Christianity and are we aimlessly rambling in a parched spiritual and moral wilderness? Does character count for many Christians? If so, why did over 80 percent

---

1. Phillips, *Your God Is too Small*, 7.
2. Ibid., 8.
3. Ibid., 18.

Introduction

of white Evangelicals vote for Donald Trump in 2016, when his actions lay bare his lack of character and his unworthiness of moral esteem?[4] This book addresses these baffling questions.

Thus, we purpose to forge a heightening, broadening, and strengthening of Christian character building upon the character of Jesus Christ. "Building" is an apt metaphor since we construct edifices upward, outward, with strength, and upon a solid foundation. Yet, "building" also implies a work in progress, and we all (especially me) are in progress, in dire need of being redesigned and remodeled. Nevertheless, our main point is to show that, for Christians, character really does matter as high moral actions flow from high moral character.

Character is strengthened in three ways: (1) modeling moral heroes by heeding their noble voices; (2) humbly recognizing our need for help; and (3) engaging in high causes for the lowly.[5] An exalted Jesus provides all three with the gravitational pull to place Christian character into a higher orbit. A small Jesus produces a weakened Christian character, dooming us to moral shipwreck. In his letter to the Philippians, the Apostle Paul yearns that "Christ might be exalted by the way I live" (Phil 1:20 Phillips).[6] This is the primary goal of every Christian. From our character—a character that Jesus himself models . . . and infuses—springs our Christ exalting actions.

If Phillips's critique remains relevant and Christianity's moral downturn is unabated, its credibility withers. He did not think this disgrace was simply a matter of rare quirks, but what he called "mass-hypocrisy."[7] The loss of moral resolve means large segments of Christianity merely vegetate in face of this century's looming crises: massive poverty, staggering intolerance, Earth's woes, and destructive violence. That's why *building moral character is a most serious call for Christians today.*

On occasion, a new building replaces an old edifice—one whose foundation is weak, whose structure is failing and no longer safe. Thus, it is necessary to clear away some of our inadequate notions of God, Jesus, and Christianity, many of which we learned in childhood. Yet, some flawed beliefs result from the human propensity to focus upon our self-interests without considering their negative impacts upon others. Christians call this selfishness "original sin" inherited from Adam's "Fall." Sin not only drives

---

4. See Bailey, "White Evangelicals Voted," 1.
5. Brooks, *The Road to Character*, 8–47.
6. On occasion we shall refer to Phillips's translation of the Bible with a "Phi" notation.
7. Phillips, *Your Jesus Is too Small*, 8.

our individual selfishness, but its off-shoots also result in the subtle and blatant cultural distortions that worm their way into every social institution, including the church, shaping their self-identity; i.e., their character. Thus, we need to reckon with *corporate* character and how that reinforces our individual character.

In this country, we battle various "Americanisms" that continually gnaw away at our higher nature and allure our lowest. We are easily hoodwinked and captivated by:

- The American Dream—we want to achieve material success and upward mobility for ourselves and our children though diligence and hard work.
- American Manifest Destiny—God granted us a special calling and moral vision to redeem this Land from its savage natives and spread its mission to the whole world.
- American Exceptionalism—our nation is morally, economically, and politically superior to any other country.
- American Triumphalism—because of our calling and sense of superiority, we are destined to impose our values of freedom and democracy upon others. Some pejoratively refer to this as American Imperialism.
- American Frontierism—our westward pioneering spirit enhanced the values of initiative, hard work, and self-reliance.
- American Rugged Individualism—reinforced by frontierism, the glorification of independence that prioritizes one's own interests without necessarily considering those of the broader society.
- American Pragmatism—what is important is what works best, irrespective of how transcendent moral principles might judge.
- American Capitalism—the unregulated ownership of private property and the means of production with a strong consumer base, but skewed to disproportionately benefit the "supermanagers."
- American Creedal Values—equality of opportunity, but not results; freedom from interference, but not from want and misery; and justice and well-being for the rich and powerful, but not necessarily for the underclasses and minorities.
- The American Spirit—those qualities that follow from the above such as self-reliance, self-interest, pragmatism, resilience, material

Introduction

prosperity, independence, persistence, initiative, competition, mobility, hard work, fame, family, and religious devotion.

- The American Character—being obsessed with one's own interests. As Naomi Klein states, "seeing ourselves as little more than singular, gratification-seeking units out to maximize our narrow advantage."[8] David Brooks, in his bestselling work on character, summarizes it as "the Big Me," shorthand for our tendency to self-aggrandize and self-exalt.[9] Ayn Rand, the atheist and the influential mother of Libertarian thinking, considers such selfishness a "virtue."[10]

These entrenched cultural forces that inevitably shape us (including our religious identity) complement and mutually bolster one another. Most have a bright side, but when overlaid by self-centeredness, they cast their dark shadows upon the good and infect our social, economic, political, and religious structures and institutions. We summarize them as the "American mindset," because they are "set" like concrete in our hearts and minds, hardening our souls. Paul uses the same language when describing those whose "minds are set on earthly things" (Phil 3:19). He calls those putting faith in their national ethos ("circumcision/Hebrew of Hebrews/Pharisee/law/zeal") as having "confidence in the flesh," a highly sin-laden condition (Phil 3:4–6).

To the degree these "earthly" customs are built upon *collective* egoism and fortified by our *singular* selfishness, they contribute to a society's Civil Religion. A false "confidence" in Americanized values inevitably warps our image of Jesus and inhibits us Christians from fulfilling our greatest desire—possessing Christ's mind: i.e., an uncontaminated mindset of the highest moral character. We languish under a culture that holds Christianity captive and serves up what Paul unabashedly calls "dung" (Phil 3:8, KJV). What a vulgar and repugnant image of a culture that soils our souls and institutions, and why one's character can collapse so swiftly.

The unrelenting forces of custom, tradition, and unquestioned beliefs—combined with our inescapable self-centered pursuits—bombard us every moment, forming our values and reinforcing our general perspectives on life, while blighting our character. Inevitably, these forces work to shape our picture of Jesus in a thousand different ways, justifying nearly

---

8. Klein, *This Changes Everything*, 460.
9. Brooks, *The Road*, 240–79.
10. Rand, *The Virtue*, 27–31.

Introduction

every convoluted fantasy and scheme devised by humankind. Indeed, Jesus' name has been associated with some of the most grisly, ghastly events in history—the Inquisition, the Crusades, slavery, war, the Holocaust, mass killings, and the suppression of women and homosexuals, to name the most onerous.

In these atrocities, the glory of Jesus has been so deeply tarnished and ravaged that we look back in disbelief and shame. I, too, remember with remorse some of the views I once held, while confessing that my assault upon his greatness and beauty still continues in subtle and possibly in blatant ways. Jesus cringes at my daily impious mockeries. It's hard to break out of culture's captivity—out of sin's fast grip and its wreckage. Yet, all Christians believe that, through God's grace and power, we can be forgiven, can change course, and can stand on a higher moral plain. Unutterable sin is covered and transformed by unutterable grace.

However, in this new age of social media and Internet access to just about everything and anyone, the American mindset is reinforced like never before, and instantly. Nothing escapes the effects of the revolution in communication, including religion. With all the discordant voices, Christianity is being propelled to a public crossroads.

Has Christianity drifted so far off course, been so scandalized, that a new reformation of Martin Luther's magnitude is a most urgent call in these days? This question compels us, like Luther, to search out the Jesus of Scripture and enter into his very heart and mind. We hope to get as close to our Lord, our Savior, and our Friend as possible; in fact, so intimate with Jesus that we become him and he of us so as to think and feel as he is. We long to have his very character within the deepest sanctuary of our souls, lighting those dark labyrinths touched by past abuses, present self-centeredness, and future ambitions. This means entering his world, walking the paths he walked, and hearing what he said to those he comforted and to those he confronted. Then, our character/conscience will be shaped by his life and teachings and be manifested in our daily walk. We will also be better able to counter the continuous bombardment of alien values.

For this reason, we affirm the Red Letter Christian movement that draws attention to the actual words of Jesus to help guide us through the many pitfalls in our ongoing journey towards God's perfect moral will.[11] This does not imply that the black letters are less important or authoritative,

---

11. Campolo, *Red Letter*, 21–29.

Introduction

but rather that Jesus' words give them meaning. Later, we shall address this issue more fully.

Significant differences separate the many brands of the Christian faith, named as Baptist, Methodist, Roman Catholic, etc. However, the chasms we shall address are much deeper than simply denominational differences. On the one side, stands my boyhood faith articulated today by slick Televangelists and found over a wide range of more Fundamentalist churches and denominations. Here theology is highly individualistic and focuses upon personal salvation, doctrinal correctness, literal interpretations of the Bible, and Conservative moral stances (especially around sexual and political issues). This form of Christianity emphasizes common fears and the self-benefits of religion to overcome those fears. It also tends to be skeptical of science, secular education, government, and international bodies. It is highly visible and influential with an ever growing number of people falling under its spell. It packs quite a wallop in the social and political realms.[12]

At the other end of the spectrum resides a less popular Christianity that understands faith in more communal terms, puts less emphasis upon doctrinal purity, interprets the Bible nonliterally, and appreciates science and secular education. It defines moral issues more broadly to include the rights of minorities, the fairness of economic structures, and promotes environmental concerns and peacemaking, to name the more pronounced. The differences in these two Christianities are not absolute, but are important enough to push and govern the divide that transcends denominational distinctions. I understand these divisions, because, at one time or another, I have wandered the territory on each side of the spectrum.

I started out on the cradle roll of the Conservative Baptist Church in a small rural community in Oregon. I attended Sunday School, morning worship, BYF (Baptist Youth Fellowship) every week, and faithfully read my Bible and prayed daily. Back then, I slavishly obeyed all the imposed social codes about not smoking and drinking and swearing and dancing and card playing and theater going and necking—the key markers of being a good Christian. One reason I chose to attend Wheaton College was its strict views on such matters.

In my hometown church, I was taught many of the notions found in Part 1 of this work, which I now regard as misguided. Much of the theology I learned was highly individualistic, negative, fear based, and personal sin focused. We were continually reminded of how straight and narrow is the

---

12. Phillips, *American Theocracy*, 171–262.

Introduction

way of Jesus, how we must not conform to this world, and how we must always come out from among sinners and be separate. Much time and effort was spent on deciphering the last days of Earth and why, for instance, a pre-Tribulation rapture is more scriptural than a post-Tribulation one. God's love was mentioned, but usually in the context of God loving sinners so that they might not perish, but believe and gain eternal life. Personal testimonies focused upon conversion experiences or how God had miraculously intervened and solved a crisis during the past week. Prayer requests addressed immediate personal problems and very seldom referenced broader community issues, much less global ones (unless we were praying for a missionary). Also, the Bible verses I memorized were highly selective, having mostly to do with the "spiritual laws" of personal salvation and only a smidgen regarding loving others, but never the many passages about seeking social and economic justice. Deeply ingrained in this approach and zealous to spread it, I felt the call to the ministry. I was ordained a Conservative Baptist minister, with my entrenched American mindset.

Looking back, I benefited by attending Wheaton College rather than my initial choice of a nearby Bible school. At Wheaton, I studied under some of the best Evangelical scholars who put me on a new spiritual path. For instance, Richard Longenecker broadened my understanding of biblical interpretation and moved me beyond Scofield Dispensationalism that had dominated my faith. My geology professor, Dr. Douglas Block, taught me to appreciate science, including the fact that Earth is more than 6000 years old and that "Flood Geology" has no credibility. Dr. Arthur Holmes showed me that philosophical reflection enhances faith.

My mind expanded at Fuller Theological Seminary, where I learned to relish New Testament scholarship as George Ladd's student assistant. Other Evangelical scholars such as Barnard Ramm, Geoffrey Bromiley, and Edward Carnell taught me the value of truth and to question longstanding assumptions that I learned in church as a kid. I have not, however, abandoned my strong view of Scripture, a stand for which my neighbor and colleague, Carl F. H. Henry, expressed appreciation in his autobiography.[13] These experiences left me an important legacy—that God's truth is the most valuable thing in the world no matter where it leads; and its pursuit is lifelong. I feel very blessed and live in deep gratitude. Most people are not given such opportunities to learn from such Evangelical giants of the faith. Yet, like all Christians, I struggle daily against my sinful self.

---

13. Henry, *The Confessions*, 330.

Introduction

Back then, Jesus was deeply concerned about what people thought about him. He pointedly asks his disciples, "Who do people say that I am?" After the disciples repeat some popular misreadings, he presses them, "But who do you say that I am?" (Mark 8:29). Jesus hopes that his followers clearly understand his identity and mission, while dismissing common misconceptions. Yet, his questions still smolder today as we continue the search for Jesus' true identity and purpose in the midst of overwhelming confusion.

This work resonates with the fact that the real Jesus, the author and finisher of our faith, continually exposes religious fraud and denounces the distorted theologies of his day—those based upon wealth, power, harmful creeds, outworn traditions, violence, and the many other faces of self-interest. Foreshadowing Jesus' prophetic mission, Luke begins the story with Jesus' dramatic challenge to the popular theology of his hometown folks, more specifically, their narrow view of "exceptionalism"—believing that God loves and blesses them more than outsiders (Luke 4:16-30). His rebuke of their collective egoism and misguided understanding of God's will is so deeply felt that the townspeople, in their rage, attempt to kill him by throwing him over a cliff.

For Luke and the other Gospel writers, this inaugural event reveals Jesus' identity—his moral character—and foreshadows his subsequent earthly mission. Thus, we revisit this incident in later chapters. It signals one reason that Jesus ultimately dies. He hangs on a cross because he rebukes home-grown theologies at every turn—theologies that, sadly, look remarkably similar to those popularized today; theologies born of time-weary traditions, misplaced fear, and ambitious rage that still mock him, crown him with thorns, and crucify him afresh. After exposing these misshapen beliefs that impugn Jesus' character and render him small, we shall show the ways to exalt him and position him on the highest moral ground.

Millions claim Jesus as the most significant factor in their lives. While we believe that his death saves us from sin and eternal abandonment, we also affirm that we should always act as he would act; always do what glorifies and exalts him and not us. We are guided in both our major and mundane life decisions by asking, "What would Jesus do?" In fact, we believe we should mimic his perfect moral life with our whole being as best we can, relying upon the Spirit's power. He is our inspiration to excel ethically and to never be content with moral mediocrity.

Introduction

It is unthinkable, then, that any Christian would deliberately belittle Jesus in any way—a grave misadventure, blasphemous, and disgraceful. Yet, assaulting Jesus' glory and majesty need not be deliberate. Simply ignoring or dismissing a large body of his teachings that counter the Big Me and our American-driven lifestyles and outlooks also make light of him. In Part 1, I tend, for the sake of scrutiny, to caricature the more popular distortions that belittle Jesus. Most of these ill-shaped beliefs do possess an element of truth, which we shall acknowledge. But overblown or half-truths are especially tenacious. They often corrupt the whole.

For example, the Mona Lisa is considered a great masterpiece of art. Pretend that someone painted a long Pinocchio-like nose on Madam Lisa. Most art lovers would consider this a breathtaking travesty and sacrilege, completely ruinous of the painting's beauty. They'd find little solace if someone pointed out that 95 percent of the work remained as Leonardo painted it. The violation taints the whole, because it was intended to be seen and appreciated as originally painted. The same holds true for our picture of Jesus. To exaggerate any one dimension of Jesus while overshadowing others is to blot his flawless image and thereby smear the whole.

Looking to his sayings and beautiful life as recollected in the Gospels and underbrushed by contemporary scholarship, Part 2 will paint a more viable integrated picture of Jesus—magnifying his person and reflecting the masterpiece he is. We hope to resurrect the loving and justice-advocating Jesus buried beneath years of misinterpretations and misdeeds done in his name. Because any picture of Jesus is subject to discoloring, we sketch him with a sense of humility and ask forgiveness when our brush strokes disfigure him. We must never forget that most good things in life can easily be misconstrued and misused, whether food, sex, or money. This includes religion and its most sacred elements. Prayer, for example, can be a powerful spiritual experience, yet could degenerate into narrow selfish petitions like asking God to provide us a new Ferrari.

Some misrepresentations of Jesus might seem unimportant. Yet, like a cancerous melanoma, what looks small can be quite serious, even deadly, if allowed to fester. On the other hand, if we obsess over minor theological points (like the nature of angels or end times), we tend to ignore the more important aspects of faith, even faith itself. Jesus rebukes people who quibble over trivial issues, while they "neglect the things which carry far more weight in the Law—justice, mercy and good faith" (Matt 23:23, Phi). The ideal is balance. To eat only desserts would be nutritiously disastrous.

Introduction

A healthy spirituality keeps all dimensions of faith in proper perspective. Adapting a popular saying: to fixate on molehills misses the mountain splendor; to make mountains out of them distorts perspective.

Hopefully, most Christians will find this book challenging and see it as an opportunity to struggle with some inadequate views of Jesus that we all embrace. Our goals are threefold: (1) to shake from our feet the dust of the worst forms of Christianity and prevent an authentic Jesus from going extinct, and thereby, muting his urgent voice; (2) to deepen our understanding and appreciation of Jesus and become more resolute to conform our character to his and follow him in biblical, uncorrupted, and credible ways; and (3) to highlight the loftier strands of Christianity for those who have discarded Jesus due to the many falsehoods accorded him. On a broader scale, we will sketch a Jesus who addresses his tumultuous world in which human sustainability hung by a thread. Given our similar predicament, we hope to convince you that his words echo with compelling relevance for today.

PART 1

BELITTLING JESUS

One of the early Christian hymns in the Bible celebrates Jesus' absolute humility, often referred to as the *kenosis* or self-emptying section (Phil 2:1–11). Jesus emptied himself of divinity, entered Earth in human form, as a humble servant, obedient to the point of dying, even on a cross. For such, God has "highly exalted him and given him the name that is above all names, so that at the name of Jesus every knee should bend . . . and every tongue should confess that Jesus Christ is Lord to the glory of God the Father."[14] Here Jesus stands not just exalted, but *highly* exalted, above everything—above all principalities and powers, even Caesar. This cosmic truth shapes the Christian community's humble response. Whom God has exalted, we bow before and confess as Lord. It's unthinkable, then, that we would denigrate him in any way, but we do so by *exalting ourselves and our selfish pursuits above him and, thus, shamefully humiliating the humble one.*

Of course, whatever we might do to tarnish his magnificence, splendor, reverence, dignity, infinite loving goodness, and unsurpassed truth could never efface his highly exalted standing one iota, since it is granted by God. Nevertheless, by exalting the self, we demean Jesus and undercut our own spirituality/morality, leaving us barren, cold, and dark. Furthermore, by besmirching his name we humiliate him before the world and make it much more difficult for *every* knee to bend and *every* tongue to confess that he is Lord.

---

14. Note that God transcends specific gender identity. Jesus and Paul focus upon "Father" precisely to undercut the ancient patriarchies where fathers acted as if they were gods and especially Caesar's claim to be the "Father of the Family." Thus, we shall retain "Father," but will use "Heavenly Parent" for contemporary references.

Since Paul wants all Christians to exalt Christ in the way they live, he exhorts us to "make sure that your everyday life is worthy of the gospel of Christ" (Phil 1:20, Phi). Christians usually emphasize believing the gospel, proclaiming it, sharing it, and defending it, but Paul's focus here is upon the *everyday living* of it. Yet, what exactly is the "worthy-life" that exalts Christ and how does it relate to his "gospel?"

Fortunately, Paul immediately provides the answer: it is the *moral life* that overflows with "love" as expressed in "compassion" and "sympathy"—the fundamental building blocks of character. Not content to simply *name* compassion as the content of character, Paul specifically *describes* it. The compassionate, "gospel-worthy life" means (1) we should not "look to our own interests, but to the interests of others"; and (2) this gospel-way sacrifices "ambitions" and humbly "regards others as better than ourselves" (Phil 2:3–4).[15] These two key ingredients of Christ-like character could not be more at odds with the American Character. A compassionate person puts aside his or her's own concerns, enters into the sufferings of others, and serves their interests. The key component of compassion is humility, the quality that squelches our selfish superior-seeking pride. A soul aflame with humility thaws the glaciered heart, frozen by self-centeredness that snuffs out the sparks of empathy. A humble character opens up the possibility of serving others.

Paul links compassion's humble regard for others to "sharing in the Spirit." For Paul, Christian spirituality is nuanced as empathetic *communal sharing*, made possible by the power of the Holy Spirit (Phil 2:1–2; see also Phil 2:12 where God "empowers you both to will and to work for God's good purposes"). When compassion is interwoven within the whole fabric of church life, it defines a congregation's corporate character, and consequently, the character of all those who participate in it. *We, then, become most Christ-like within a loving community.*

When Christians in community are "of the same mind" or unified in regarding others first, they then have "the same mind in us that was in Christ Jesus."[16] Paul's dream, and that of every Christian, is to be so saturated, so interwoven with the mind of Christ that Jesus' love fills every cell of our brain, every vein to and from our heart, and every recess in our soul. His

---

15. Note that some translations have "look not to your own interests *only*," implying that one should consider their own interests on par with the interests of others. This rendition waters down Paul's moral imperative. The NRSV drops "only."

16. See 1 Cor 2:16 where Paul also says Christians possess "the mind of Christ."

personhood becomes our personhood, his loving character our character. In his voice, we find our soul's true voice. By using the phrase "in us," Paul reinforces his view that the mind of Christ is primarily a *corporate, public* mind penetrating every policy and practice of church and communal life, including the behaviors of cultures, systems, structures, and institutions.

The word "mind" in "mind of Christ" means more than simply "intellect," but rather intelligent moral makeup or character. Paul "prays" for the Philippians that their "love may overflow more and more with *knowledge and full insight* to help you determine *what is best*" (Phil 1:9, italics mine). For Paul, when love and wisdom are linked they enhance one another and lead to the best moral outcomes. "Mind," then, is that *assemblage of virtues ratified by reason*, corresponding to what we mean by "moral character." Jesus, backed up by Paul, provides Christians with those specific moral qualities and their enlightened applications that constitute a person or a nation of high character. We shall name and explore those qualities in Part 2.

Paul's purpose is to *uproot the aggrandizing, status seeking ethos of Adam's sin that distorts our character*. He chastises Christians who "proclaim Christ out of selfish ambition." Such persons are "the enemies of the cross of Christ"; they make Jesus small. In contrast, he commends those who "proclaim Christ out of love and goodwill" (Phil 1:15–17; 3:18). Unfortunately, the American mind or character based upon the Big Me, the "me-first-self-exalting" narcissistic philosophy, and its "virtue of selfishness" morality, has seeped into a popularized American Christianity. *Most of the distortions surrounding Jesus we outline below are created by excessive self-absorption reinforced by the American temperament.* Paul's blunt description of his day as "a crooked and perverse generation," well applies now (Phil 2:15). Simply put: the American mind with its cultural mandates is at war with the mind of Christ and we, including the church, need his moral character instilled within us if we are to stand united and strong. The mind of Christ rends the veil of blindness and deafness toward the interests of others and the crises facing our world.

Given the tenacity of the sinful human plight, how can Paul motivate Christians to overcome callous indifference or from "growing weary in doing what is right" (Gal 6:7)? How are they able to live the life worthy of humble self-giving; i.e., to possess the mind/character of Christ? He makes a most powerful appeal: "the *gospel* of Christ." But what is it about this good news of Christ that moves and sustains us? First, Paul reiterates that the good news Jesus taught is about love's compassion. When Christ's character seeps into our minds, this love comes alive "within us" and we emerge from the shell of self-absorption.

Second, due to egoism's unrelenting power, Paul does not simply *exhort* us to live the self-emptying compassionate life. He pulls out all the stops and *motivates* us, with a most compelling *action narrative* in hymn form that celebrates the moral beauty of Jesus' own humble self-emptying through his incarnation. The melodic moral truth here is virtually inconceivable—that a divine being would give up divine prerogatives, become a lowly human, lower yet a slave, even lower to die, and the lowest of all to die most shamefully on an imperial cross. This downward plunge can only be described as infinite and *all for humanity's interests alone*. What a breathtaking descant of humility *for us* who live amidst the clangs and gongs of self-enhancing gaudiness. We are so seized by the wonder of it, that we are *inevitably* awakened to passionate kindness. That's very good news for us, for others, and for Earth.

Paul appeals to Jesus' example elsewhere: just as "Christ did not please himself," so also we should not "please ourselves. Each of us must please our neighbor for the good purpose of building up our neighbor" (Rom 15:2–3). He also references Jesus' incarnation to ending economic disparities since Jesus' "generous act" of giving up riches to become poor, we, by his poverty, might become rich (2 Cor 8:9). The connection between Christ's unalloyed character and Christian character is clear-cut—*a blending of minds to serve the needs of others*. By its very nature, compassion is "incarnational"—the humble action that "in-fleshes" ourselves into suffering servanthood as Jesus did, and then bears the everyday scorn, the helplessness, the anxiousness, and the longings of the downtrodden. Jesus *shows us* what he expects us to become—to switch our self-mindfulness for *his* other-mindfulness of humble self-sacrifice. As Luther admonished, we must become "little Christs" and proclaim aloud Jesus' compassionate voice in order to continue the work where he left off.

Yet, Paul reminds us: lest we think that giving up a little ambition and a miniscule of self-interest for others is so magnanimous, we utterly pale at the astronomical self-emptying Jesus has done for us. Furthermore, since Christ's gesture begins in heaven, the values he brings are cosmic, universal, absolute, the highest, and the best. He brought something native from heaven with him, the surge of eternity's sacred watchwords, an inheritance for all people—humility, love, and compassion—the foundations upon which character is built. They stand above every transitory cultural value, determining to what degree all lower values are judged. Thus, for instance, self-reliance, normally an offspring of pride and a compassion killer, is transformed into a reliance, not for one's own benefit, but rather *to meet the suffering neighbor's need.*

More is at stake here for Paul's understanding of the good news. Jesus is not only the flame that sparks our compassion, but also *our Savior from its lack*. His death created our possibilities. That he sacrificed much makes it possible for us to do even a little. Thus, when Jesus is humbly acknowledged as our Savior, we are asking him to deliver us from our innate self-centeredness, from the Big Me, to reclaim us from cultural conformity, and to shape us in his image of compassionate humility. No other depiction of compassion's route that follows from Christ's redemption could be so profound, so compelling, and so transforming. The difficult part is being shaped and molded in the face of powerful negative forces, and why we continually need the Spirit's empowerment to transform our minds into the fitting temple of Christ's mind (1 Cor 6:19).

This inseparable connection between Jesus' death and character change (both individual and corporate) is often missed or underplayed by Christians. Most misinterpretations of Jesus mentioned below spring from either neglecting the ethical dimension of Jesus' incarnation and death on the cross or else distorting that ethic by embracing selfish non-compassionate values that are not gospel worthy. Ironically, the self-centered vices that sent Jesus to the cross are the very sins for which his death atones. How awful that we so humiliate Jesus and sully his Lordship and its good news by exalting those death-dealing values in our walk and talk, as we shall see below.

Thus, Paul reminds us that in a balanced Christian view, the exalted Jesus Christ is confessed as both Savior and *Lord*. Since lordship implies eternal, transcendent, divine status, accepting Jesus as Lord assumes that we overthrow all our false transitory cultural "lords," that we conform to his divine image, and that we follow his eternal model of humble other-directed-self-emptying *as all part of salvation's package*. In addition, the new birth brings about Jesus' Lordship over *every* dimension of our lives. He is Lord of our outward looking social, economic, and political selves, and not simply our inner psychological self (the inner life). To exclude his Lordship in any one area creates counterfeit lords (idols) to whom we inevitably bend our knee and worship.

PART 1—BELITTLING JESUS

These pseudo-lords, that reign over us personally and corporately, can be material (always wanting more), social (climbing the ladder of status and fame), or ideological (extremist values and views). They can be addictive and are reinforced by the American Character. When they are turned into objects of Christian worship, the most bazaar expressions of faith emerge. As one observer suggests, these "overlords" are pushing some Evangelical congregations into cult-like practices.[17] The distortions of Jesus we address below prompt the question, "Who is lord?" In muscling out Christ's lordship, Jesus becomes little and irrelevant. However, Jesus and Paul assure us that all the false gods we are prone to exalt will ultimately crumble.

For our purposes, a critical distinction emerges from Paul's phrase, "the gospel of Christ." Is it the "good news" *from* Jesus or *about* Jesus? In his inaugural hometown talk, Jesus quotes from Isaiah and identifies his prophetic mission as "anointed to bring *good news* to the poor . . . to proclaim release to the captives and recovery of sight to the blind, to let the oppressed go free, . . ." (Luke 4:18; Isa 61:1, italics mine). Here the gospel *from* Christ is the good news about transforming the miserable conditions of people. This message governs the Jesus story in the Gospels and why they are called "Gospels" and why Paul links the good news to the worthy-life of compassion.

Early on, however, the Christian Church underscored the gospel *about* Jesus and shrunk that to his atoning death for our sins. While this highlighted a key Christian truth, it tended to relegate the collection of Jesus' life and teachings simply to "introducing" the cross. The church's most famous creeds (Apostle's and Nicene) that define what is essential to faith and the enduring yardsticks of orthodoxy celebrate his birth by the Virgin Mary, but then skip to his suffering and crucifixion under Pontius Pilate. Unfortunately, his everyday humble obedience to God's will in serving humanity through love, his healing of very sick people, his feeding of those starving, his condemnation of wealth, his acceptance of outsiders, and his eschewing of violence are left unstated.

In fairness, these creeds arose due to specific christological controversies with deep political ramifications. Actually, Christians went to extreme measures to follow Jesus' teachings, and the creeds refer to him as "our Lord," although they do not define his lordship. Nevertheless, these "timeless" creeds inadvertently bequeath a muted voice; a legacy that the sayings and actions of Jesus are not that important for a confessing faith.

17. Molineaux, "Could Your Evangelical," 1.

What really matters is his atoning death on the cross.[18] Paul corrects this lack when he connects Jesus' incarnation, life, obedience, and death with our orientation toward the interests of others. The Apostle makes the same link elsewhere by declaring, "I have been crucified with Christ, and it is no longer I who live, but it is Christ who lives in me" (Gal 2:20). "Cruciformed" Christians are those in whom Christ's self-giving mindset governs their every action *in identification with his humble servant-obedience and his sacrifice for humanity on an imperial cross.*

Since the ancient creeds excluded the good news *from* Jesus, Christians are left picking and choosing buffet style from the Gospels whatever satisfies their sweet tooth, leaving the more nutritious morsels untouched. Many misshapes of Jesus catalogued below result from ignoring or disliking his heaven-sent ideals. We all could think of a mandate or two that makes us, especially we Americans, uncomfortable: "go sell all your possessions and give the money to the poor"; or "it will be hard for a rich person to enter the Kingdom of heaven"; or "lend, expecting nothing in return"; or forgive "seventy times seven"; or "if you are angry with a brother or sister," it is "murder"; or "everyone who looks at a women lustfully has already committed adultery with her—in his heart"; or "love your enemies"; or "love your neighbor as yourself" (Matt 19:21, 23; Luke 6:35; Matt 18:22, 5:22, 28 Phi, 44; Mark 12:29–3l). Most of us squirm under these "hard sayings" and when we add them up, it's surprising that anyone in our Big Me society likes much of anything Jesus has to say. His radical egalitarian love is the highest bar for anyone to reach.

Indeed, some relegate his tough commands to a future "Kingdom ethic," irrelevant for us now. Jesus, however, spends his whole mission inaugurating the Kingdom *now*, defining its moral parameters, and calling people to repent and enter it. He disputes with opponents over what is important and unimportant for entering it, and many found his ideas unacceptable, even blasphemous. That does not stop him. He prioritizes values and reinterprets texts in ways he believes ought to mark the true Kingdom/spiritual quest in the present and into the future.

Another reason Jesus' specific teachings have been minimized grows out of the Enlightenment distinction between the Jesus of history and the Christ of faith. Some scholars argue that much of the Gospel record is not

---

18. Contemporary confessions now include the life of Jesus such as that of the Presbyterian Church (USA): "Jesus who proclaimed the reign of God; preaching good news to the poor and release to the captives; . . . healing the sick and binding up the brokenhearted, eating with outcasts . . ."

reliable history, but skewed by the later beliefs and issues facing Christian communities. Thus, the only "facts" we can know about Jesus are his zeal for and radical obedience to God; and these attitudes are what Christians should emulate.[19]

While all Christians must be zealous and radically obedient, recent new "quests" for the historical Jesus suggest that he provides us more specific moral direction.[20] *His moral truths cannot be left out of the preached gospel from and about him.* A gospel that ignores his compassionate responses leads to "cheap grace, the deadly enemy of our Church" as Bonhoeffer has so famously remarked. "Costly" discipleship leads us to emulate the loving demands listed in the Sermon on the Mount.[21] Jesus' dying upon the cross for our salvation not only frees us from our sinful ingrained cultural values, but allows God to brand in our minds and write upon our hearts the values Jesus taught (as Jer 31:33 predicts). When we ignore or oppose his work and moral truths, we not only disgrace grace, but we also cheapen him.

Paul's counsel to regard others better than ourselves follows from Jesus' instruction to "lay down one's life" for others when the embers from hell blow their way. Then, we model Jesus who admonishes us to "love one another as I have loved you" (John 15:12–13). We deface God, the gospel, and God's love in salvation history—Jesus Christ—when this radical teaching on unconditional love does not become central to salvation, faith, and Christian behavior. Put in classical terms, Justification and Sanctification are only transforming when inseparable. Slighting his agenda at any point leads to the many distortions that prevail under the guise of the gospel. It permits a lower self-minded faith to dilute our faith in Jesus' higher neighbor-mindfulness. Accepting *all* of Jesus' recorded life and compassion-shaped-statutes are essential to strengthen our character and live the gospel-worthy life.

Accepting Jesus, then, means we must *apply* his values within *every* dimension of our lives. This includes uncovering the sins and the Americanized counter-values, often hidden in religious garb, that tempt and seduce us daily. In the past, when I saw a person without a home in scruffy clothes holding a cardboard sign pleading for a dollar, I would hold him in contempt. That was due to my ingrained values like "self-reliance," "cleanliness

---

19. Bultmann, *Jesus and the Word*, 77. More recently Aslan, *Zealot*, xxx.

20. See Wright, *Jesus and the Victory of God*, 83–124; Keener, *The Historical Jesus*, 196–302.

21. Bonhoeffer, *The Cost of Discipleship*, 45, 117–220.

is next to godliness," "if you won't work, you shouldn't eat," or "he'll just buy liquor." This made it easy to label "them" with slur words like "bums," "vagrants," "transients," "hobos," "drunkards," and "panhandlers." I have since been convinced that succumbing to these prideful, heartless values chips away at the compassion Jesus taught and modeled. Yes, Paul, for instance, promotes hard work, but for the purpose of having something to "share with the needy" (Eph 4:28).

Let's go back to our image of Pinocchio, whose nose grows due to his habitual falsehoods. When he lies to the good fairy, his nose grows so big that he gets stuck in the room. This metaphor speaks to the seriousness of distorting the truth in the presence of the Higher Power, or even in God's name, including the name of Jesus. We become even more imprisoned within our relentless ego-concerns because we tie them to the powerful hold of religion. The analogy also warns that a misshapen Christianity can become virtually cartoonish.

John the Baptist once said of Jesus, "He must grow greater and greater and I less and less" (John 3:30, Phi). We have gotten it backwards—we attempt to make ourselves bigger and bigger, and thereby, Jesus becomes smaller and smaller. Hopefully, this work will put us all on guard against a deformed Christianity that belittles Jesus, disparages his mission, tarnishes and withers our spirituality and character, and causes others to disdain his holy and exalted name. As the poet Shelly once said, "The corruption of the best produces the worst."

Regarding America's piety, one social commentator observes, "An uninstructed and unreflective Christianity has indeed taken hold of the population."[22] That's because those who shout the loudest and pander the most get heard, however bizarre and ugly their message; and they are defining present-day Christianity—a cultural Christianity that has lost its way and treads a pathless morality. The Apostle Paul describes them as ministers of "trickery" and "crafty in deceitful scheming"; those who "pervert the gospel of Christ"; and who "by smooth talk and flattery deceive the hearts of the simple-minded" (Eph 4:14; Gal 1:7; Rom 16:18). Unblushingly, they reduce faith to a vulgarity, a darksome charade, a hideous sham, with their unseemly ravings. They spread their nets far and wide, snaring the easily deceived and beclouding a Son-lit Christianity. It is frightening what marches, without shame, under the banner of Christianity. Many people are left wondering, what, after all, is true religion as opposed to a gnarled

---

22 Robinson, "A Proof," 18.

misrepresentation? Some have been so thoroughly brainwashed, they may never see the difference, unable to distinguish between wheat and tares, between truth and big fibs. This misshaped Christianity, upheld by fraud, cannot go unchallenged.

Most significantly, the standard and ever present TV preachers, who many consider the face of Christianity, come off as hypocritical-scandal-ridden-money-making-show-business hucksters, as fake as TV's "professional" wrestlers. In one survey, these religious mega-personalities are rated as the least admired, even less than prostitutes and used car salesmen. They only score higher than drug dealers and crime bosses.[23] These charlatans of the faith survive by repeating trite stock phrases, catchwords, and meaningless clichés. Doing the Devil's deeds, they flatter the basest passions and milk the most gullible, focusing more on the dark purposes of attracting donations than credibly expounding upon the ministry of Jesus. Sadly, Christianity is then ridiculed as escapist, navel-gazing, blessings-all-mine, judgmental, macho, warmongering, vengeful, anti-science, anti-woman, holier-than-thou, capitalistic, eco-destructive, blindly patriotic, intolerant, and "wing-nutty."

This ubiquitous popular Christianity, associated with the lowest common denominators in the spiritual quest, *must not prevail*. It is not only theologically outrageous, but may also lead to unhealthy and sometimes disastrous consequences. The big loser, of course, is Jesus whose image and moral authority is not only sacrilegiously stained, but routinely trashed. The Lord's name is being taken in vain, and not just with everyday curse words, but by the obscene ways he is portrayed. To borrow from Ecclesiastes, the misuse of his name has become a "vanity of vanities"; i.e., the greatest of vanities.

Studies show that a large number of young people are shunning organized religion, which does not bode well for its future.[24] They see Christianity as either irrelevant to the major issues of the day or else it takes the wrong side of those in play. The religion that many see portrayed in the media seems reactionary and out of touch with their highest aspirations. They stand aghast as Jesus gets dragged into the crassest expressions of faith and practice that exploit fear, revere outworn creeds, and justify self-absorption. His name becomes associated with crackpots like Jim Jones, Timothy McVeigh, David Koresh, and Fred Phelps of Westboro Baptist Church to

---

23. Patterson and Kim, *The Day America*, 141–45.
24. Putnam and Campbell, *American Grace*, 120–33.

mention the more visible and grotesque. Atrocious villains can be clothed in Sunday suits. Add to this: book burnings, anti-Semitism, racism, genderism, homophobia, homelessphobia, Islamophobia, climate change denial, and the unwelcoming of immigrants. In the public consciousness these negative images and attitudes that inevitably affix to Jesus soil him, discredit his message, and make Christianity seem farcical and easy to spurn.

Let's look at some ways the Big Me mentality and the American Character whittle Jesus down, leaving him to cast a scant shadow of his real self.

1
A Simply-saving-souls Jesus

An all-pervasive distortion of Jesus sees his mission as simply saving souls from the eternal torments of a fiery hell in order to spend the hereafter in heaven's bliss. This belief virtually defines Christianity in America, especially within its more Evangelical wing. Certainly, a basic faith-claim is that Jesus Christ came down from heaven to die on the cross as our substitute in order to save us from that eternal separation traced to humanity's mutinous dawn. Yet, was his primary mission simply to save individual souls? And did he promote the notion of an inescapable eternal fiery afterlife? And what were his views on heaven? We shall explore his soul-saving mission in this chapter and his take on hell and heaven in the next two.

For many Christians, evangelizing, or converting sinners, is a key component of their faith (thus, the name, "Evangelicals"). Of course, evangelizing is not an effort limited to religious people. Every advertisement in the media tries to convince us to buy its product. In all honesty, I hope to convert you, the reader, to what I consider to be a more credible view of Jesus. So what is the problem with all the "Jesus Saves" signs that crop up at our roadsides or in our ballparks?

Wars have been fought over the proper understanding of salvation and the atonement. Possibly most theological debates hinge on the doctrine of salvation (soteriology): who is saved, how are we saved, from what we are saved, and for what are we saved? The "from" part is usually answered as being saved from sin and ultimately from its consequences—eternity in hell. However, what we are saved "for" is often blurry. Are we saved simply for heaven? Are we saved for some arbitrary do's as opposed to sin-laden don'ts, for some generalities like living for Christ, for a set of religious practices like attending and working in church, reading the Bible daily, praying, evangelizing the unsaved, or other disciplines? These questions touch upon the character of God and humanity, the role of the Holy Spirit, the nature of the church, and who makes it into heaven or not. Most importantly, one's notion of salvation affects our understanding of Jesus' life and death. Our views of redemption either magnify Jesus or potentially cheapen him and his mission.

For most, proclaiming the gospel or good news focuses primarily upon the individual's acceptance of what Jesus did on the cross for him or her. The most well-known Bible verse sums it up: "For God loved the world so much that He gave his only Son, so that everyone who believes in him should not be lost, but should have eternal life" (John 3:16, Phi). Many have applied this verse to individual salvation only. However, it also points to God's love for the "world"—for the cosmos as a whole (including, but not limited to, humans). The individualistic perspective underplays God's love for broader social communities in the plan of salvation. Moreover, overwhelming institutional powers may be prime contributors to one's inner chaos, to one's acts of desperation, to one's erecting false gods and addictive substitutes—to one's need for deliverance. On the other hand, broader community forces, such as the church, could help to usher in salvation's healing power.

The motto of the seminary where I taught was "The Whole Gospel to the Whole World through Whole Persons." A Saving-souls-only Jesus is the Jesus of a partial gospel, to a partial world, through a fragmented person. Richard Stearns, President of World Vision, reminds us that we leave a huge "hole" in the whole gospel by limiting salvation to individuals alone and not seeing its public dimensions.[1] This lack undercuts Jesus' message and ministry in a number of ways.

First, the focus upon personal salvation finds more traction from American individualism rather than from the biblical faith. As previously mentioned, religion reflects a particular society's cultural ethos. Certainly, the American experiment of promoting the individual's inherent worth is a great moral and political achievement. However, America's "rugged" individualism looks beyond the human dignity issue and promotes the predominant world ethos of the self as a "singular gratification unit." The focus upon the individual provides little motivation to sacrifice some self-interest

---

1. Stearns, *The Hole in Our Gospel*, 2.

PART 1—BELITTLING JESUS

for greater social causes. The cooperative virtues, like compassion, wane. Furthermore, self-orientation also feeds personal pride, historically regarded as a deadly sin. Thus, when religion cozies up to individualism, it enters a seductive egocentric chamber that scandalizes Jesus. It then becomes a Big Me religion in contradistinction to Paul and Jesus' worldview of humble other-directedness.

Second, reducing Jesus' mission to saving souls tends to downplay his prophetic role. The prophets speak of salvation in national terms. Jeremiah longs for the "salvation of Israel," and talks about Judah and Jerusalem "being saved" (Jer 3:23; 4:14; 23:6; 33:16). Isaiah, too, voices a "redeemed" Jerusalem, Israel, and Zion (Isa 1:27; 44:23; 52:9). At Jesus' birth, the prophet Anna announces the Christ Child to people eager for the "redemption of Jerusalem" (Luke 2:38). Then, after Jesus' death, two of his followers express the hope that he would "redeem Israel" (Luke 24:21). Jesus often delivers his salvation message to groups of people like "the poor," "this evil generation," and "Jerusalem, Jerusalem" (Matt 5:3; Luke 11:29; 13:34).

That Jesus presents a broader holistic view of his salvation message is reflected in his Kingdom policies. His speech in Nazareth begins with, the Lord "anointed me to bring good news to *the poor*. He has sent me to proclaim release to *the captives* and the recovery of sight to *the blind*, to let *the oppressed* go free, . . ." (Luke 4:18, italics mine). His message addresses socially, economically, and politically affected *groups* of people, those destined to history's oblivion. This inaugural speech governs his mission activity to the very end—to rally the hope-fed dreams of the underclasses.

Unfortunately, Christians often interpret his Nazareth sermon in non-prophetic psychological terms such as living in *spiritual* poverty—blinded, oppressed, and held captive by personal sin. However, throughout his mission, Jesus reinforces the point that salvation casts a broader net. In his Judgment of the Nations speech, it is *nations* that are redeemed from judgment based upon whether they provide social and economic safety nets to "the least of these," i.e., their most vulnerable citizens (Matt 25:31–46). Clearly, in this last and his early Nazareth speeches, Jesus attests that corporate entities can be and need to be saved.

Third, the Simply-saving-souls Jesus rests upon a view of sin that understates its nature, power, and extent. Indeed, Jesus wants to save us from all our past and present personal sins (when we sorrowfully confess and do not cavalierly continue in them). All our individual sins, whether trivial or truly heinous like murder, child molestation, and pillage bear social consequences, some punitive, even though God will forgive the sinner.

Yet, as horrendous as individual's sins might be, sins can become more monstrous when incarnated into structures, systems of ideas, and political values, often in mutually reinforcing ways. It was because of the corporate culture of preserving an institution's reputation at all costs that child molestation persisted within Penn State, the Boy Scouts, and the Roman Catholic Church. The "macro-sins"—atrocities committed on a grand scale such as slavery, genocide, obliteration bombing, great social and economic gaps, and the environment's destruction—have found their home, strength, and legitimization when embedded in corporate structures. Historically, Christianity is not blameless in reinforcing these sins. In fact, it could be argued that the one reason some Christians focus upon individual salvation is to leave structural evils untouched. This allows them, for instance, to deplore personal racial attitudes, but ignore institutional racism.

The King James Version reinforces the narrower view by describing the Kingdom as "within you" (Luke 17:21). While Jesus wants us to fully embrace the Kingdom notion in our hearts and minds, he did not mean that the Kingdom is purely psychological—one that deals exclusively with a person's inner soul. Newer versions translate the phrase as "among you" which correctly underscores its outward and community reference.

That Jesus' "Kingdom of God" (a slogan he uses over 90 times) refers to broader social/political/economic realities rests in the term "Kingdom" itself. In his day it could only mean one thing—"government"—a political term and not simply a religious one. A well-regarded Evangelical scholar insists that ignoring the political and economic dimensions of the Kingdom is to "falsify" and "belittle" it.[2] Jesus derives the phrase from the longstanding Jewish belief in the reign of God, not just in the lives of individual Israelites, but *over the nation as a whole*. The "of God" phrase implies governing grounded in God's divine character of true justice, freedom, and shalom. Thus, the phrase "Kingdom of God," is best translated today as "Good Governing."[3] Jesus feels called to deliver Israel from the injustices, oppressions, and violence of Roman occupation and bring about a good form of governing, sparking the disciples' hope that he would redeem Israel (Luke 24:21 with Ps 130:8, where the nation is redeemed "from all its iniquities").

---

2. Borg and Wright, *Meaning of Jesus*, 219.

3. See Miller, *Jesus Goes to Washington*, 41–50, for a discussion of the "Kingdom of God" being translated as "Good Governing."

Repentance and salvation, then, address both sin-laden people and their flawed institutions that wreak massive social and economic havoc. The Simply-saving-souls Jesus never adequately acknowledges the fact that millions are born into structurally-induced poverty amid circumstances that provide few options and that crush opportunity. Salvation includes deliverance from the economic and political evils that crush people.

In Jesus' form of governing, we need redemption from all artificial self-centered markers belonging to Caesar's Kingdom and all other imperial systems: birth lineage, social standing, wealth, misused power, and ritual. To reject or ignore this broader truth diminishes his teaching about salvation and does a great disservice, not only to him, but to all people living within faltering or failed governments. This also leaves Christians with a shriveled character that looks little beyond itself. As a side effect, structural sins often breed escapist notions of religion that fortify other disfigured views of Jesus, like a Magical-thinking, a Quick-fix, or a Prosperity Jesus.

In summary, Jesus awakens not only individual faith, hope, and love, but also *civic* faith, hope, and love. His salvation reaches to the devastating macro-sins that transcend any one person and that have wormed their way into cultures, institutions, and political and economic systems. Yes, he looks for individual change of heart and redeems us from our addictions to status-seeking and possession-hoarding and, when these are frustrated, anger's rage. However, he also sees the necessity for broader change in mores, structures, laws, and policies that feed and perpetuate personal sins. When we give all our attention to repentance from individual sins and do not call for institutional repentance from its mega-sins, we are allowing unchecked calamity to befall humans and Earth. In doing so, we puncture the gospel and deflate its scope and power. It shrivels the gospel, leaving a truncated, belittled Jesus in its wake.

2
A Fire-escape Jesus

The popular view that Jesus came primarily to save souls raises the question, "From what is our soul saved?" Often the answer is that we are saved from the *penalty* of sin that results in death and the eternal torments of hell's fiery fury. Here, the primary motivation to be saved springs from fear.

Fear, a powerful motivation and survival mechanism, is programmed into the foundational structures of every animal's brain. It is necessary and good; for without it, human risk-taking would know no bounds. We educate our children early about life's perils: hot stoves, busy streets, strangers, playing with matches, guns, and much more. When we see them engaging in risky behavior, we sternly warn them, "That could hurt you." Development theory suggests that children learn early to make moral decisions based upon fear, either from the natural consequences of their actions or being chastened for them. Later, they act upon other factors such as the willingness to please, respect for authority, the promises they have made, etc.[1] Some people seem to be fearless, others are shaken by very slight dangers and, in fact, many (maybe even most of us) live with irrational fears called phobias. While not always at the surface, fear, which is grounded in our basic self-regard, lurks nearby and snakes its way through much of our decision making . . . and our prejudices.

Fear has always played a prominent role in religion. Religion emerged as a survival mechanism, especially around the growth and distribution

---

1. See Kohlberg, "Moral Stages," 34–35. Kohlberg posits six stages of moral development, the highest being acting from "universal moral principles" (like Jesus' Golden Rule).

PART 1—BELITTLING JESUS

of that which is most basic to life—food. With the rise of civilizations, the ruling elites, claiming god-like status, used the fear of the gods to ensure that the peasant farmers willingly brought a percentage of their crops and livestock to the ruler's central storehouses. In return, the priestly notables guaranteed that the gods would grant the peasants both fertility and *personal immortality*. Many of the earliest rituals and sacrifices were designed to placate a god's chastising anger for noncompliance to elite demands, both now and in the afterlife. And if the prospect of future misery failed to convince, then leaders held a strong trump card—the fear of military might. This scheme reinforced extreme social and economic inequalities in the ancient world.[2]

Immortality and the uncertain prospect of a dreadful afterlife also invaded Christianity. Dante graphically described it as the torments of roasting forever and that's how medieval art most imaginatively pictured it. In his famous sermon, Jonathan Edwards portrays sinners in God's angry hands dangling over hell's ovens. The fear of spending eternity in a fiery furnace with its 24/7 excruciating pain has been a successful evangelistic tool. As Pascal famously noted, it's a safe wager to embrace Christianity rather than risking even the slightest chance of landing in such a dreadful place. In accepting Jesus, one escapes eternal damnation. Many, including myself, became Christians largely to evade this ghastly, unthinkable fate.

The bullies of fear who pitch hell's fury paint Jesus in the image of a strict parent God, extremely harsh and vengeful, ruling with a big stick, easily angered at the slightest misbehavior, ready to abandon sinners, and pitilessly watch them burn and writhe forever if they do not repent. They quote biblical passages where a seemingly punitive Jesus speaks of the final judgment: where "every tree that does not bear good fruit is cut down and throw into the fire"; where the rich man died and ended up "in Hades where he was being tormented . . . and in agony in these flames"; where offenses lead to "the rubbish heap, where decay never stops and the fire never goes out"; where one is "banished to the darkness outside, where there will be tears and bitter regret"; and where compassionless nations face "the abyss" and "eternal fire prepared for the devil and his angels" (Matt 7:19; Luke 16:23–25; Mark 9:44–48 Phi; Matt 8:12 Phi, 25:4; Luke 8:31; Matt 25:41). For villages that refuse to welcome Jesus' disciples and their message of good governing: "it will be more tolerable for the land of Sodom and

---

2. See Becker, *Escape from Evil*, 4–5.

Gomorrah on that day of judgment than for that town" (Matt 10:15). On the surface, these words and images seem harsh and unrelenting.

The book, *Love Wins*, created a maelstrom of controversy for suggesting that Christians re-examine their view of hell, given the infinitely loving God.[3] Some have accused the author of being "unbiblical"—the kiss of death within Evangelical circles. How might we deal with hell in light of God's love?

The answer boils down to how we interpret the Bible and how we look upon the character of God. While our beliefs are biblically based, we should not assume that every passage is to be interpreted literally (literalism feeds into the many flawed views of Jesus discussed below). To exaggerate the point, when Jesus exhorts us to "go and do likewise" in the Parable of the Good Samaritan, he does not expect us, when coming across a bleeding man in our setting today, to literally find some wine to pour on his wounds and round up a donkey to transport him to the nearest Motel 6. Such literalism would be grossly stupid and irresponsible (although in a rural area of a poor country, it might be taken more literally). In our day we would call 911 or perform other contextually appropriate actions.

We should exercise caution, then, when speaking of a literal hell, an abode about which the Bible overflows with picturesque language, rich in time-bound metaphors and analogies. It all began in the original paradise, where the drive to take everything, including godlike power, *banished* humans from the Garden. For Jesus, hell depicts what happens to those *outside of or banished from God's dawning Kingdom*, which includes the *banishing of ruinous values*, since they have no place in the coming Kingdom (the renewed paradise). These "evildoers" and their values are "thrown out" of the Kingdom, where they are destined to the hellish "weeping and gnashing of teeth" (Matt 8:12; Luke 13:27–28). Jesus' imagery of hell as outer darkness, an abyss, a bottomless pit, an eternal fire, a garbage dump, and Hades, if taken literally, are incompatible. How does outer darkness harmonize with a fiery furnace, and how do these images square with a bottomless pit and a Greek Hades?

We should question, then, whether Jesus believes in a forever fixed punishment—torturous beyond our imagination. In truth, breaking rules does have consequences and retributive justice is necessary within any viable human community. Jesus believes in the Mosaic Constitution; and his Sermon on the Mount is filled with renewed legal rulings to help stabilize

---

3. Bell, *Love Wins*, 63–94.

deteriorating village life impacted by Roman imperialism. His judgment sayings listed above are primarily directed against the imperial ethic that allows governments and their leaders to ignore the poor, the hungry, the strangers, the unsheltered, and the ostracized. Hell speaks of the demise and banishment of bad leaders who create a hellish Earth and why they are excluded from heaven's Kingdom that brings relief.

Jesus paints these graphic apocalyptic pictures of final judgment to grab the attention of anyone violating God's commandments. By turning up the heat, he hopes to make them *literally* sweat (fear has some value). The Book of Revelation stands as the prime example. It contains a simple straightforward message that could be reduced to one easily dismissed sentence, "Very bad things will happen to leaders who defy Jesus' Kingdom teachings, while good things come to those who observe them." The writer, however, imaginatively dresses this statement with multiple graphic and terrifying images like the sun being darkened, the seas turning to blood, mountains falling upon people, horsemen bringing famine and destruction, and on and on for twenty-two eerie chapters that rival any sci-fi world-ending movies today. In fact, some of Hollywood's most terrifying apocalyptic films have taken their cue from the Book of Revelation.

Revelation's graphic language, however, is mostly symbolic and meant to impact the reader at the deepest emotional level, to loosen despair's tight grip, and bring hope and jubilation to people mistreated by Rome, the gluttons of carnage. Yet, it directs judgment and instills the gravest anxiety against nations and hellion leaders who have oppressed the downtrodden and treated them mercilessly. Apocalyptic language is subversive and intends broad social and political change, radically and quickly. Hellish governing will come to naught and disappear. Apocalyptic imagery does find its relevance today as governments become hell-bent on stockpiling weapons of mass destruction and are cavalier about overheating the Planet.

Jesus, like all the prophets, spoke of judgment because he understood the destructive power of vice. When he tells his disciples that if villages do not live the Torah they will end up desolate like Sodom and Gomorrah, he foreshadows hell on Earth. In other words, hell happens within fallen social and political institutions: when minorities are open game; when obliteration bombs explode over villages; when school girls are abducted; when escaping immigrants die in the seas and the desert; when pink slips are handed out and homes are foreclosed; when air becomes unbreathable and water turns foul; when people rot in prison; and when pity ceases. Jesus provides an escape from all these and the other "hells" on Earth, but only if people and powers emulate his character and follow his loving ways.

One's assumptions behind a literal hell, as well as other flawed views about Jesus, follow from seeing God as stern, shrill, and vengeful; whose wrath floats to the top and whose love and forgiveness sink to the depths. The great achievement of the Bible is its portrayal of God as approachable, who hears cries, sees suffering, and knows misery—an empathetic and compassionate God who takes the side of the marginalized and brings judgment upon those leaders who cause them harm. So dramatic is this change in God's essence/character that "forever and for all generations" God wants to go by a new name, "Yahweh" (Ex 3:7-15, 6:2-9, 33:17-20). The Bible then understands God as unquenchable love who remembers sins no more (I John 4:8; Jer 31:34, also quoted in Heb 8:12). Like God, Jesus exhorts us to forgive unendingly (the meaning of "seventy times seven" [Matt 18:22]).

Thus, God's wrath could never be God's essence or character since it lasts but a moment. What endures forever, what defines God's character, is *steadfast* love (Ps 30:5, 118:1). God chastens in order to serve loving purposes. God's forgiveness is what reigns (Heb 12:6). The belief in a literal torturous hell is incompatible with this more compassionate parent-like picture of God and Jesus. It is hard to image that any loving parent under any conceivable circumstance would ever condemn their own child to eternal torture. And God's love is infinitely superior to even the most profound love of a human parent, no matter how much God hates sin.

Fear of damnation should never edge its way to the center of faith and govern our spiritual life. If anything, Christians should harbor a godly fear of hell's incendiary embers that blow into people's lives daily—fearing the torments that befall them and our Earth. We should also fear our complicity in stoking hell's flames and be motivated to repent and change course.

Jesus, during his last agonizing hours, prays, "My Father, if it is possible, let this cup pass from me; yet not what I want but what you want" (Matt 26:39). Jesus accepts his "cup" for the sake of *our* redemption. This cup also signifies that Jesus "descended into hell" (the creedal formulation) which probably meant the abode of the dead. Paul too, for the salvation of his kinsfolks, wished himself "accursed" (another image for hell) and cut off from Christ (Rom 9:3). What an extraordinary mark of character—to risk, not only his life, but also his own eternal destiny for the salvation of others. Another example is the martyr Dietrich Bonhoeffer who believed in pacifism. Yet, out of his love for humanity and his hope in God's grace, he joined a plot to kill Hitler, believing it important to wrest the steering wheel from a madman driving into a crowd of innocent people, even though it meant "great guilt."

Jesus predicted that "the love of many will grow cold" (Matt 24:12). Ironically, coldness brings hell's scorching coals upon us and upon others. God's judgment is love's chastisement to bring repentance and build character. But seeing Jesus as one's escape hatch from an eternal inferno is to belittle him and cheapen his view of judgment, his forgiving character, his inspired mission, and the faith he engendered. Thus, when someone utters the common profanity, "God damn . . . ," it is not simply using God's name in vain, but also an obscene theological half-truth that sullies the Heavenly Parent's character and, likewise, that of The Son.

3
A Pie-in-the-sky Jesus

We have already touched upon an inadequate view of salvation that centers upon escaping from hell's horrors. However, what about those who see salvation primary as a guarantee of heaven's haven? Scripture does speak of a future state of eternal bliss for those who endure the sufferings of this world. The desire for a utopian paradise, like its counterpart, eschewing hell's fury, is a powerful religious motivation and an effective evangelistic tool. For many, "going to heaven" is not only the final spiritual goal of the Christian life, but its supreme one. They embrace and worship a Ladder-to-heaven Jesus. Their faith is pejoratively referred to as "pie-in-the-sky," a phrase that parodied the popular hymn line, "In the sweet by and by, we shall meet on that beautiful shore."

Since the first traces of religious experience, a core feature has been the longing for immortality or "eternal life." Unfortunately, the prospect of life beyond the grave has been used by the powerful to control and exploit the masses. As noted above, the rulers created cults (like Baalism) and promised people bounty and immortality *if* they fill the storehouses of the elites (much like prosperity preaching today). It should be noted that in the Bible, "eternal life" refers to the *quality* of life and not the *unending span* of life.

But should the prospect of a heavenly paradise be the primary motivating factor in our Christian lives? Is this not another aspect of religion wrapped in self-centeredness? Is not the Christian hope more profound than simply anticipating some "mansion over the hilltop?" And should we even assume it is somewhere distant and non-terrestrial? Yet, what about those who allege to have been there and back?

PART 1—BELITTLING JESUS

Those claiming a Near Death Experience (NDE) subscribe to a literal heaven or at least an afterlife. Eben Alexander III, a neurosurgeon, wrote a best-selling book, *Proof of Heaven*, where he claims to have seen heaven and God during a deep coma. Another book, *Heaven is for Real*, describes heaven's visit by a four-year-old boy Colton, the son of a pastor, who saw Jesus and conversed with long-deceased relatives.

The Bible is relatively silent on the nature of heaven and its whereabouts. Indeed, most of Jesus' talk is Earth oriented with *heaven coming to us* and bringing those values enshrined by eternity that will transform us and our world. He declares in his famous prayer, "your Kingdom come, your will be done, on Earth as it is in heaven" (Matt 6:10). Matthew not only substitutes "heaven" for "God" in Jesus' Kingdom formulation because of the Jewish reticence of saying God's name, but also because the Kingdom represents heavenly or eternal values (God's will) invading Earth.

Heaven is where you "store up for yourselves treasures" or values that really matter as when Jesus says to a rich ruler, "Sell all that you own and distribute the money to the poor and you will have treasure in heaven" (Luke 18:22). He instructs his disciples to "sell your possessions, and give alms . . . , an unfailing treasure in heaven" (Luke 12:33). These God-like economic policies for the poor have heavenly or transcendent and enduring significance. The Christ-worthy life here on Earth is defined by our accumulated *moral* treasures that represent the best in human character and action. Although Jesus promises a paradise, fixating upon getting to a non-terrestrial abode not only reflects sowing treasures for ourselves, but sees Jesus primarily as the means to future rewards, giving rise to the popular ditty, "you can become so heavenly minded that you are of no earthly good."

In his famous prayer, Jesus sees heaven storming Earth as the Kingdom restores humanity's (Adam's) lost earthly paradise. Just as hell brings its imperial devastation to Earth, heaven brings a Kingdom with its medicine to heal. Simply put: heaven is everything that happens inside the Kingdom of God, just as hell is everything that happens outside it. Any time God's will is done on Earth, heaven occurs and hell has a setback. The Book of Revelation vividly reinforces the view that heaven is here: the throne of God comes down accompanied by the New Jerusalem with its imagery of pearly gates and streets of gold and its power to heal the nations (Rev 21–22:7). This echoes Jesus' teaching that heaven comes as a down-to-earth political entity—a Beloved Kingdom—that models the loving will of God.

An exalted Jesus provides us the light to discern what is heavenly and what is hellish on Earth.

Thus, we should view with some skepticism those in comas who claim ascent to heaven and conversations with God and dead relatives. First, we must be careful not to impose Greek dualistic notions upon Christianity, one being that of disembodied spirits. This contrasts with the Hebraic holistic view of the mind/body that, for instance, drives Paul's opposition to the Corinthian dualist's belief in an out-of-body resurrection (1 Cor 14:38–41). Dr. Alexander's experience relies heavily upon this separation of mind and body, more at home in the Eastern Religions.

Second, these experiences are highly subjective, reflecting the subtle intricacies of the human brain, subject to hallucinations, visions, and dreams, especially when under the influence of medications and stimulants. Chemical imbalances in the brain can drive people "out of their mind" and cause them to lose complete touch with reality. Moreover, the brain is very tricky and can distort what we see. During a deep coma, like Dr. Alexander's, brain waves may be flat, which leads him to claim that an out of body experience cannot be attributed to brain games. In response, the time period of entering into such a coma or coming out of it does allow gradual brain activity and the possibility of hallucinations, which could explain Dr. Alexander's experiences. This is also true of a child's imagination in Colton's case. Furthermore, we might normally expect a nonbeliever's NDE to be that of hell rather than heaven, unless, of course, God is a God of many chances which I believe is the case.

Thirdly, we live in a culture saturated with the paranormal. The so-called "History Channel" gluts it programming with sightings of flying saucers, ghosts, aliens, UFOs, and Bigfoot. One channel aired a series on "miracle resurrections." Society is also drenched in religious symbols and ideas, so that even a nonbelieving surgeon knows that God permits evil due to human free will—a truth he claims was revealed to him in heaven. He also calls God "Om," a well-known spiritual symbol in Eastern religious traditions or it could reference the Western idea that God is omnipresent, omnipotent, etc. Also, Colton's experiences reflect traditional and common Sunday School images, such as God sitting on a throne and a European looking Jesus. Positively, good can result from NDEs as in the case of Dr. Alexander. He discovered that we need to get in touch with our spiritual side, become the person God intends us to be, and manifest love and compassion, "the very fabric of the spiritual realm."[1] In the end, this is what Jesus attempts to get across about heaven—the inspiration to make way for heavenly, loving deeds here on Earth and not become obsessed with fanciful out of this world speculations.

In the end, whether or not a future non-terrestrial heaven and hell exist, the devoted followers of Jesus are not primarily concerned about fearing future punishment or the prospect of heavenly rewards, features which reside at the lowest level of human self-centeredness and at the lowest stages of faith and character development.[2] Christianity is not the only culprit here. Think of all the violence committed because someone hopes to get a tent full of virgins in paradise. This reprehensible theology makes Mohammad quite small. Indeed, as we grow "to maturity, to the measure of the full stature of Christ," our character will develop (Eph 4:13). We are then driven to selflessly work to eliminate the present hellish injustices that plague people. We then support others to experience the heaven they dream, if they can still dream. This means moving beyond a Fire-escape, Pie-in-the-Sky Jesus, which diminishes him and his mission of bringing heaven's eternal self-emptying values to Earth.

---

1. Alexander, *Proof*, 85.

2. Fowler, *Stages*, 244–45. For Fowler, by reaching the sixth or highest stage of faith, we see ourselves as members of the broader compassionate community.

4
A Prosperity-sugar-daddy Jesus

For some, faith not only brings future bliss, but also present material "blessings." They perceive Jesus as a Sugar-daddy, ready to hand out material sweets upon request. Certainly, Jesus is concerned about life's basic necessities. He decries the poverty and injustices that lead to lingering human misery. His mission is to serve those lacking basic survival needs. While Jesus believes, "One does not live by bread alone," he also instructs people to pray, "Give us this day our daily bread," or enough to keep us alive (Matt 4:4; 6:11). However, accumulating more and more, way beyond material sufficiency, is a persistent and powerful force in American life, virtually programed into our DNA. Our insatiable appetites reinforce a selfward looking spiritually that expects divine handouts.

People gain self-worth, even identity, by the stuff they possess. Sociologists call it "conspicuous consumption." Our salvation through things addicts us to hoard the latest and the best (even spawning a reality TV show on hoarding). However, what we think a headrest is but a pillow of thorns that ultimately bursts our fragile bubbles. We are obsessed with excess; and even Christians are infected with this disease. Prosperity preaching contributes to and legitimizes crass materialism by calling it "God's blessings." Unwittingly, it buttresses the pernicious human flaw of greed that the church has historically labeled a deadly sin. How destructive our unquenchable desires can become is documented on the non-stop episodes of TV's *American Greed*. A corollary is the Santa Claus Jesus, meting out gifts based upon whether one is naughty or nice, even though Jesus taught that God "makes his sun rise upon the evil and the good, and sends his rain on the righteous and the unrighteous" (Matt 5:45).

PART 1—BELITTLING JESUS

    Many preachers, especially Televangelists, shape their whole ministry around a theology and ethic that highlights material wealth. In worst cases, they beg and beg for funds with slick "seed" money gimmicks, promising that when people give to their ministry, God guarantees material abundance in return. They often link a believer's commitment to Christ with shelling out money to them. These preachers feature personal testimonials about God sending buckets of cash in return for one's "faithfulness" (meaning: they gave generously to the evangelist's cause). The techniques are high-powered, persistent, and guilt-inducing.

    While watching a prosperity preacher one night, I held momentary hope when he exhorted his viewers: "We should never seek prosperity, only Jesus." Unfortunately, he followed up with: "When you seek Jesus, prosperity follows." How can this theology be any more contrary to Jesus' spirit? Jesus calls a hoarding rich man a "fool," while leavening a moral truth: "Be on your guard against all kinds of greed; for one's life does not consist in the abundance of possessions" (Luke 12:13–21). Those who have, often covet much more. The fool pawned his soul, his spirituality, for the trifling—the eventual rubble in a landfill. Jesus surely grieves when we portray him as a prosperity peddler that guarantees a life of wealth, ease, and merriment.

    Some "Christian" TV programs, like *The Jim Bakker Show*, prey upon our stockpiling impulse. The program is not much more than an extended infomercial, selling products such as generators or years-long packaged food supplies. To add theological insult, they hawk these products out of survivalist fears that the world is falling apart, and one must prepare for the near-at-hand last days. Other TV Evangelists will provide "miracle spring waters" or "Psalms 91 oil" that has been "prayed over 17 days." Their guarantees of prosperity are reminiscent of the phony snake oil salesmen during the frontier days.

    A most egregious and extreme example of prosperity preaching occurred when a TV Evangelist shared that she looked up and saw a cloud in the form of a camel. This was God's sure sign to tell her viewers that their camel was coming in. She explained that the camel represented abundance, prosperity, and money and noted that the camel can carry 800 lbs. Thus, 800 lbs. of material goods could come to those watching the show. She further noted that because Jesus promised to restore everything before he comes again, he has promised to restore all their wealth, 800 lbs. worth, before the end times. What she said next did not surprise me. Every person should send her ministry a tenth of 800 lbs. or eighty dollars as the "seed" to their prosperity. Of course, she also pleaded for those who could to send in the full 800 dollars as their seed.[1] Such outrageous "seedy" gimmicks occur almost daily on the religious channels.

Given the Americanized values listed above, we can understand why the Sugar-daddy Jesus retains such a hold upon American Christians. Add Calvinism, with its doctrines of predestination and election that considered prosperity as the sure sign of one's predetermined salvation. The thrift and hard work this engendered is dubbed "the Puritan ethic," which contributed to Capitalism's rise.[2] Here Jesus is assumed to be perfectly at home with all the values undergirding a freehanded capitalistic economic system, which savors the unlimited accumulation of riches for some while permitting relative poverty for others. Prosperity thinking undergirds the American Dream of owning a nice home (maybe a second home on a lake) and a fancy car or two and all the material conveniences and luxuries that snowballing indebtedness can buy. Our hoarding instinct subsidizes the myriad of storage units that dot the American landscape. The values of self-reliance, rugged individualism, and cutthroat competition further reinforce prosperity thinking.

The theology behind prosperity was famously propounded by the Gospel of Wealth advocate, Andrew Carnegie. He believed that the "laws of civilization" endow certain people with "superior wisdom" to generate (and distribute) wealth. Russell Conwell, a Baptist minister and founder of Temple University, popularized the prosperity gospel in his "Acres of Diamonds" sermon, which he preached over 6,000 times. Conwell claimed that God raises up a few godly people, entrepreneurs, gifted to create wealth and drive the engine of commerce. Poor people are poor due to their own shortcomings.[3] This view gave divine legitimacy to a capitalistic-oriented economy and very rich CEOs. It finds moral traction in "the profit motive" and "the bottom line" thinking, lofty guises for individual and corporate selfish pursuits.

The Garden of Eden story holds the ultimate clue as to why we are easily seduced by wanting more and more. Genesis is a remarkable commentary on the glory and the perversity of human nature and how easily our majesty can serve vice. Adam and Eve are created with the freedom to make rational choices and are mandated not to consume everything in the

---

1. Dr. Williams, Oct 13, 2013, on the Word Channel.
2. Weber, *The Protestant Ethic*, 155–83.
3. Conwell, *Acres*, 27–56.

Garden. However, they fall for the character-killing Big Me lie and take whatever is "a delight to the eyes" under the illusion it will bring happiness and god-like status—deformities stamped forever upon their minds. The story's enduring truth is humanity's unquenchable desire to relentlessly take in order to enhance one's standing (hence, conspicuous consumption). It finds its imperial shape in palaces and temples.

Yet, this grim Genesis narrative gets worse. When frustrated, brother (Cain) overpowers and kills brother (Abel), and thus, initiates the deadly spiral of bloodletting that saturates the pages of history. Freud named this dark side the "id"—the immediate gratification and destructive impulse. Christians call this gloom that hovers over the human prospect, "original sin." The serpent, then, is no accidental tempter in the human story. It symbolizes what governs the most basic part of the human brain called the limbic system, a system that, ironically, we share with reptiles. It triggers the survival functions, determining when to take flight or when to stand and fight; it is obsessed with self-preservation. All living creatures instinctively watch out for themselves, and in humans this translates into a never-ending quest for gold, glory, and the resultant gore. The ancient fertility myths (like Baalism) preyed upon guarantees of fertile wives, livestock, and crops in return for "offerings" to the rulers.[4] From times beyond reckoning, religion and selfishness have mated, yielding a theology driven by the assumption, "God will surely bless you if . . . ." Prosperity preachers seem closer to these ancient character-crushing fertility cults than to the Judeo-Christian ethic.

In a remarkable twist on our egocentric instinct, the Hebrew Bible calls us to redirect this powerful drive toward *our neighbor*, pursuing their interests with the same vigor as our own. Thus, "you shall love your neighbor *as yourself*," a command Jesus calls the "greatest" (Lev 19:18 with Matt 22:39–40). Can you imagine what a better world this would be if we were as obsessed with another's well-being as we are with our own; that we would consider another as number one as we do ourselves? This "as yourself" inevitably transforms our innate selfishness into thinking of others' interests even *above* our own—what Paul promotes as the true character of Christ which we should emulate (Phil 2:3–4).

Certainly, Jesus wants everyone to flourish and prosper and does not wish anyone to grovel, starve, and live without clothes and shelter. He promises these necessities when he says, "Set your heart on God's kingdom and its goodness and all these things will come as a matter of course" (Matt 6:33,

---

4. Becker, *Escape from Evil*, 44–62.

Phi). Good governing will provide one's needs. Jesus, however, does not tolerate greed-based-get-rich-quick schemes or great economic gaps. He criticizes people for loving and worshiping money since it is a false god he calls "Mammon" (Matt 6:24). By posing the rhetorical question, "What will it profit them to gain the whole world and forfeit their life?" (Mark 8:36), he makes it clear that the quest for material wealth is not only quenchless and futile, but also destructive to the human spirit, besides harming others and Earth's ecosystems.

Thus, Jesus requires the rich to "go, sell what you have and give the money to the poor" and tells the story about a rich man who ends up in Hades because he will not share even a crumb with a houseless man groveling at his doorstep (Mark 10:21–23; Luke 16:19–31). For Jesus, hoarding wealth in the midst of poverty is sinful, because it creates that poverty. He warns, "A camel could more easily squeeze through a needle than a rich person get into the kingdom of God" (Matt 19:24). He tells a parable about the "lure of wealth" which is a thorn that "chokes the word" from ever bearing fruit (Mark 4:1–20). These references and many others counter any concocted view that Jesus promises material wealth and that prosperity is a sign of God's pleasure.

Given Jesus' censure of wealth, it's breathtaking how prosperity preaching is so prevalent today. In America (and everywhere), money talks. Because churches are dependent upon healthy giving, they tend to cater to the whims of the wealthy. Many Christians are drawn to tout the economic, political, social, and ecological beliefs of the rich, such as less tax for the wealthy, fewer regulations on business, less inheritance tax, less entitlements for the "lazy" and "undeserving" poor, yet more bailouts for large corporations—all ways that perpetuate large economic gulfs and undercut character building. To assume that Jesus brings material prosperity to some while others languish only cheapens his message.

Doubly unfortunate for those living at life's margins, just barely surviving, is that they often blame themselves, while desperately latching onto any thread of prosperity's false hope. A credible Christianity; however, assures a heavenly stored eternal "wealth" of good works and rejects a greed-based-get-rich-quick morality. When the quest for material prosperity takes center stage, Jesus is mocked and we render him ever so meager.

5
A Sentimental Jesus

A heaven-looking faith might encourage some Christians to see Jesus in highly emotional and overly nostalgic ways. Certainly, feelings and personal recollections play a valid and important part in all religious experience. Christianity cannot be reduced to heartless rationality nor can it divorce itself from the yearnings of past experiences. Undoubtedly, one of the reasons Christianity survived was because of the "enthusiasm" or charisma manifested by the early church.[1] Raised in this daunting scientific and technological age, we may need stronger doses of emotion to become more human. More than occasionally, misty eyes might do us well. The feeling of compassion contributes to our spiritual growth and moves us to the most humanitarian acts of self-giving. Emotions are powerful, yet volatile; they can cloud our judgments and, when uncontrolled, lead to mayhem and "crimes of passion." Emotions can be easily manipulated and exploited by the unscrupulous.

Emotions, like painkilling medicines, become addictive when over prescribed. For some, the spiritual life becomes a journey into a nostalgic, long gone, and mostly irrelevant past, an extravagantly gushy inconsequential present, or an unhitched-from-reality future. When such feelings play a predominant role in shaping one's faith, they produce a Sentimental Jesus—a "feel good" Jesus who soothes and comforts, but seldom challenges. Just repeating the name of Jesus with intense emotion gives some people a spiritual high.

1. Käsemann, *New Testament*, 104.

A Sentimental Jesus

Those who take the sentimental journey with Jesus find difficulty in adjusting their faith to the challenges of changing times. Since their religious experience is glued to past forms, they may, for instance, have difficulty in adapting to contemporary styles of liturgy, music, and worship. Many American hymns were written in the Romantic period and are deeply maudlin. A sampling: "Take the name of Jesus with you, Child of sorrow and of woe; it will joy and comfort give you . . ."; "Tell me the story of Jesus, . . . Sweetest that ever was heard"; "Jesus is tenderly calling you home . . ."; "Perfect submission, all is at rest, I in my Savior am happy and blest . . ."; and "How Sweet the name of Jesus sounds in a believer's ear! It soothes his sorrows . . ."

John Newton's *Amazing Grace*, a hymn that Christians know by heart and probably Christianity's most famous, highlights the enduring power of sentimentality. "Amazing grace how sweet the sound that saved a wretch like me." "How precious did that grace appear, the hour I first believed." Contemporary Christian music also speaks of the "Gentle Shepherd" and "There's a sweet, sweet Spirit in this place." The Christmas message languishes when "Away in the Manger" sentimentalism takes over and obscures the harsh political realities surrounding Jesus' birth and what he would eventually confront. Like many of the other distortions of Christianity, a mushy faith stays inward, looking to its own sensibilities rather than directing our feelings in service to others.

A Sentimental Jesus is especially problematic because unscrupulous preachers prey upon peoples' susceptibility to melodrama. Religious hucksters, with their weepy, soppy theatrics, devoid of spiritual substance, exploit sentimentality, especially in their appeal for money. Emotionalism renders people more defenseless and gullible, believing whatever they are told, no matter how off base theologically or otherwise. The Charismatic movement is especially susceptible to an overindulgent gushy emotionalism.

Whereas the many spiritual gifts that Paul lists have as their purpose to serve others, some contemporary Christians see them as signs of their own inflated spirituality. Speaking in tongues has become the hallmark signature gift for most Charismatics. They see it as a "second baptism," and the highest step on the Spirit-filled ladder, even though Paul listed it last (1 Cor 12:30). When addressing the proto-Gnostic misuses of glossolalia, Paul emphasizes that spiritual gifts "build up" the church rather than "puff up" individuals—his subtle chastisement for self-centered misuse and what he believes distinguishes Christian charisma from pagan ecstasy. He

PART 1—BELITTLING JESUS

discourages tongue speaking since outsiders would think it "unintelligible," "mindless," "childish," "psychotic," and "barbaric," and thereby discrediting Jesus' mission (1 Cor 14:4–26).

Fortunately, with today's sophisticated recording devices, tongue-speakers can be scientifically scrutinized to see whether they speak in a language unknown to them or even in any known language at all. Phonetic research yields that English tongue speakers haphazardly mix up the common English phonemes, resulting in simple gibberish—a combination of emotionalism and babble or "baby talk" (which does bring psychological benefit).[2] Glossolalia can also be taught to non-seekers as Marjoe Gortner, the famous child evangelist, did with the film crew that documented his life.

A retreat into an emotion-ridden Jesus tends to inhibit common sense, reflective faith, and humility. A corollary is low appreciation for facts and reason, diminishing the Lord of Truth. Furthermore, if glossolalia is of such overarching spiritual import, we would expect the most Spirit-filled person in history, Jesus Christ, to have spoken in tongues and to have encouraged it. The record is silent.

Sentimentality tends to counter Jesus and Paul's call to be other-oriented. One may identify with the cute little rescued lamb Jesus cuddles in his arms in the famous painting; or that Jesus alone walks with us and talks with us as we come to the dew-dropped rose garden. Both of these images, and many others like it, speak only of comfort, which Jesus surely brings. However, they obscure the fact that Jesus also challenges us to face the world we are destined to serve. What are the dangers that the stray lamb faced and how should one fend against these dangers? When Jesus walks and talks with us, what does he have to say to us about how to love our neighbor and make this a better world? These are the critical questions that are often left unanswered in the sentimental approach, because they are not seen as that important.

The Sentimental Jesus, then, does not ask much from us, except our feelings. Emotionalism is often reinforced by outworn clichés such as "Jesus never fails," or "Jesus will get you through the darkest night," or "Jesus brings perfect peace," or "put it in the Lord's hands," or "the Lord willing," and so forth. On occasion, Jesus does get emotional, but directs it toward challenging sentimental attachments to the most sacred objects in the Jewish faith. For instance, he rakes the Torah over the coals regarding retaliation and

2. Samarin, *Tongues*, 2.

does not spare the Temple system with its Sabbath and purity codes (Matt 5:17–48; Luke 21:5–6). Jesus' disciples follow him due to their commitment to his radical, dangerous Kingdom program and not for some sentimental attachment. Jesus had little use for a maudlin faith that inhibits character formation. We belittle him when emotionalism reigns.

6
A Stained-glass Jesus

A sentimentalizing faith is likely to box Jesus within church walls, experiencing him most significantly during the hour or two on Sunday mornings (or Saturday nights). Many Christians worship a Stained-glass Jesus by default, based simply on long-standing traditions. They fulfill their Christian duties by attending a service once a week in his honor, singing a few praise songs about him, by listening to prayers in his name, by reading responsively some sayings by him, by hearing an enlightening sermon about him, by taking communion to commemorate him, and by giving a few dollars to please him. All of these and many other commonplace church activities are important, beneficial, and may enhance spiritual growth, but many remain marks of what sociologists call "religiosity." Following Jesus means much more.

Limiting our faith to church activities ignores our Monday to Saturday "worship" (meaning "service") in the midst of everyday life (see Rom 12:1–2). Moreover, people may attend church for a number of reasons, religious or otherwise—out of habit, to make business contacts, for political reasons, or to scope out a potential mate. They also may be searching for a church that reinforces their already inadequate beliefs such as a Fire-escape Jesus, a Pie-in-the-sky Jesus, or some other cheapened Jesus.

As the phrase "stained glass" implies, some believe that Jesus is appropriately worshipped when surrounded by the awesome architectural beauty of magnificent cathedrals. Certainly God has created humans with boundless imagination and appreciation for art, whether in the form of architecture, painting, sculpture, music, poetry, etc. These will always remain an essential medium to deepen faith. Thank God, much of the Bible is written in poetic form. Aesthetics enhances human well-being by appreciating Creation and all that is therein, including the many marvelously artistic depictions of Jesus.

Yet, for Jesus, beauty is ultimately found in the truth and goodness that beauty conveys. When a woman washes his feet with perfume, Jesus says, "She has performed a good service for me" ("good" [*kalon*] also means "beautiful"). The beauty of this unnamed woman's act inspires Jesus to honor her with a lavish everlasting tribute (Mark 14:6–9). The structure of an act shaped by loving kindness is where true beauty is found and mirrors heaven's glory.

When Jesus prays to his Father *in heaven*, he demolishes the view that God's dwelling is confined to the Temple building or Caesar's palace, even though these were wonders of the ancient world. While God can be experienced in church structures and its rituals no matter how traditional, ornate, and adorned, God also transcends them. The Gospels record two detailed instances of the adult Jesus entering a place of worship and both events incite lynch mobs. The first time his prophetic preaching so outrages his hometown friends and relatives, that they drive him out of the synagogue and try to kill him (Luke 4:28–30). The last time, called the "cleansing of the Temple," creates such turmoil that it leads to his execution (Mark 15:11–15). Jesus refuses to be intimidated by majestic centers of worship with their exclusive, exploitative values. Rather, from his higher moral beauty, he challenges their unsightly pillars of ingrained collective egoism and cold creeds.

For the prophets of old, religious rituals retain their splendor only *within a moral framework*. Thus, Isaiah redefines fasting to mean feeding the hungry, bringing the homeless into one's home, and loosening the bonds of injustice (Isa 58:6–7). When a scribe recognizes that the love God/love neighbor command is "much more important than all the burnt offerings and sacrifices," Jesus answers, "You are not far from the Kingdom of God" (Mark 12:33–34). Amos considers it an affront when leaders seek God in places of worship yet routinely cheat the poor (Amos 5:5). Jesus calls the Temple a "den of robbers" and predicts, "Not a single stone will be left standing on another; every one will be thrown down" (Mark 11:17, 13:2, Phi). Aesthetics must serve the Kingdom of God; i.e., how God wills all people to live together and flourish in peace and love and mutual sharing. Jesus worships an unconfined generous God who makes "his sun rise upon the evil and the good, and sends rain on the righteous and on the

PART 1—BELITTLING JESUS

unrighteous" (Matt 5:45). This beautiful teaching of nature's marvels undercuts any attempt to limit God's work to inflexible exclusive institutions and its rituals.

Paul calls a Christian community "*ekklesia*" (assembly). These "churches" were modeled after Jewish synagogues and Greek assemblies where both political decisions and religious worship occurred. For fear of secretive political activities, Rome would only allow these "assemblies" to exist as civic organizations that plan monuments and events to glorify Rome and its emperor. Paul, however, has a more subversive purpose as reflected in their original religio-political purpose. He hopes to create mini-Kingdoms of God in preparation for God's coming to overthrow Rome's reign and its values. Contrary to Roman harshness, the church's strong character results in caring for one another, tearing down all the cultural barriers that give certain persons higher status, sharing their resources with one another, and renouncing violence—all for the sake of equality and mutuality (Gal 3:28; Acts 2:43–47; 2 Cor 8:13–15).

Thus, Paul, following Jesus, defines "spiritual worship" as not being conformed to this world (Roman values), but rather as a mind-renewing discernment of God's will that presents one's body a sacrifice for others (Rom 12:1–2). The character of the community of believers (the church) is destined to model what God intended for all humanity—to be one family, treating each other as family members, as brothers and sisters who sacrifice self for one another. Rome cringes at this direct attack on its values, and thus, its very existence. No wonder Paul is arrested so often and finally executed.

One church puts it accurately with a driveway exit sign: "The worship service has ended; now your service begins." Jesus realizes the limitations of rigid institutional structures and rituals and how easily they could be perverted. He tells a parable about two temple bureaucrats who pass by a dying man, presumably because aiding him might interfere with their "churchly" duties (Luke 10:25–37). Jesus sees his mission much broader, plunging into the daily affairs of hurting Galilean peasants and opposing the darksome imperial policies mediated by Rome's Temple-state surrogates. He sends out his disciples to villages to bring peace (shalom), or the overall welfare to hamlets crippled by unemployment, land foreclosures, hunger, and death.

Today, his Kingdom building activities define the character of Christians and the mission of the church, challenging what goes on in board rooms, back rooms, and war rooms. Positively, a church's character and its beauty are judged by what it provides for its *non-members*. We stain the name of Jesus and the beauty of Christian character when we focus upon routine church activities or rituals that do not champion his broader role and vision.

7
A Doctrinaire Jesus

From Christianity's birth, defending proper doctrine has played a key role. Paul's letters boil over with controversy surrounding correct beliefs vs. emerging distortions. Many disputes revolved around observing certain Jewish laws and whether Gentiles should observe them, especially the practice of circumcision. Later, groups fought over the nature of Jesus, whether he had a physical body or only seemed so, or was he simply a human, or was he both fully God and fully human. Holding sound doctrine regarding the essentials of the faith is certainly important to any religion.

Nevertheless, dangers lurk over what doctrines are considered essential and how easy one can slide into a close-minded dogmatism. Christianity leaves a corrosive legacy in fights over "sound doctrine" and orthodox purity. Early on, the church codified proper doctrine into creeds, some of which are still recited weekly in many churches. However, some Christians differed and were branded as heretics or apostates, which—most ominously—left torture, execution, and warfare in its wake.

Yet, doctrinal intolerance and its bad blood still plague Christianity. Dissenters face censure or defrocking by ecclesiastical courts, banishment from the community, and excommunication. The theological doctrines of God, Creation, Sin, Salvation, Christology, the Church, and Eschatology can be interpreted in a myriad of nuanced ways that could cause long lasting antagonisms and church splits. Even the first page of the Bible has left Christians hopelessly divided over whether God created Earth 6,000 years or billions of years ago. And the disputes continue unto the Bible's last pages where some are deadlocked over whether Jesus is coming again before or after the Tribulation.

A Doctrinaire Jesus

A spin-off of the correct doctrine approach is the obsession with "apologetics," the need to defend or prove Christianity against all assaults, especially those leveled by the "New Atheists" Sam Harris, Richard Dawkins, and Christopher Hitchens. While Peter tells us we must "always be ready to make a defense . . . for the hope that is in you," he continues by saying it is "good conduct" or "suffering for doing good" that puts the adversaries to shame (1 Pet 3:15–17). Given the difficulties of "proving" issues surrounding faith, our best defense (and maybe the only defense) is the weather-beaten good we do by defending the rights of the poor and the marginalized. The Bible says "God is love" and no Atheist in the world can deny love's existence, only its lack. It is better if Christians spend time proving God's existence by manifesting loving justice and not by getting bogged down in endless fruitless debates. Furthermore, the New Atheists often hone in upon and castigate the worst expressions of religion, many of which we critique in this book.

A most contentious debate among Christians, and one that feeds a more doctrinaire outlook, surrounds the nature of biblical inspiration. Some believe God has dictated every word to passive receptive writers (the doctrine of verbal plenary inspiration). Here, the Bible is absolutely true, contains no factual/scientific errors or contradictions, and is authoritative at every literal point. Those who hold a more open non-literalist view of Scripture, such as the Bible is true in matters of faith and practice, are looked upon as compromising biblical authority and no longer trustworthy. We must, however, be cautious with the phrase "biblical authority" for a number of reasons.

First, those who spout this phrase assume that their literal interpretations of the Bible are "cut-and-dried" true. We might call this the "Nicodemus Syndrome," as he was puzzled about the phrase "born again," thinking it meant literally going back into his mother's womb (John 3:4). Some refuse to appreciate the vast array of images in the Bible or ignore the ongoing debates over principles of biblical interpretation (hermeneutics). Thus, anyone who disagrees with their textual renderings is seen as rejecting the Bible itself. Just repeating the phrase "biblical authority" translates to "I am right and you are wrong," which, of course, shuts down all discussion. Furthermore, those who employ the phrase usually promote a "selective" biblical authority that supports their own immediate agenda.

Second, those who appeal to biblical authority assume that every Bible verse carries equal authority, a view that the Bible itself rejects. Jesus, the

PART 1—BELITTLING JESUS

Christian's ultimate authority, considers some literal interpretations nonauthoritative. Regarding the law of retaliation: "You have heard that it has been said, 'An eye for an eye and a tooth for a tooth.' But I say unto you, Do not resist an evildoer" (Matt 5:38–39). He also rejects narrow literal interpretations of the law. "If you are angry with a brother or sister," or "If you insult a brother or sister," or if you "say, 'You fool,'" you are guilty of murder. Concerning adultery, "Everyone who looks at a woman with lust" violates the Seventh Commandment (Matt 5:21–30). In these and other instances, the living Word interacts with the written Word and expands their meaning in light of contextual realities. Since Jesus is the Christian's final authority, we must attune ourselves to follow *his* mind in these matters. Later, we shall examine this matter further.

Although a man of truth, Jesus never promotes dogma in defining his mission. Rather he often breaches the walls of transmitted certainty. The most dogmatic beliefs in Jesus' day were the Sabbath laws. Everyone was expected to reverence them; their violation was a capital crime (Num 15:32–36). One day, Jesus' disciples pluck ears of corn on the Sabbath and are roundly accused. In response, Jesus comes up with an example of when David's army, out of hunger, entered God's house and unlawfully ate the bread of the Presence reserved only for priests. He then declares, "The Sabbath was made for humankind and not humankind for the Sabbath" (Mark 2:23–28). His point is that doctrines are not true for doctrine's sake, but true when interpreted to meet basic human needs.

Jesus understands that dogmatism is the stepchild of human pride—the unshakeable assurance that one's views are unerring. Its opposite is humility, the basis of character. Jesus reinforces the prophetic exhortation to "walk humbly with your God" when he says, "For all who exalt themselves will be humbled and those who humble themselves will be exalted" (Mic 6:8 with Luke 14:11). Every day Jesus comes up against doctrinal arrogance by state bureaucrats who see him constantly violating their cherished beliefs. Jesus insists that God does not judge us on the correctness of our theological doctrines. Rather, God holds us accountable for how our doctrines humble us and aid us in loving God, showing "mercy," and doing "good" to people in need (Matt 12:1–8; Mark 3:1–4). Persons of humble character, never flush in assurance, are always open to growing and maturing in their faith and to modifying outworn, inadequate, or even false beliefs. Furthermore, they do not use doctrine to club others into submission. Failure to embrace the humble spirit is to betray the truth, and ultimately, to betray Jesus. It leaves him languishing in frozen belief systems and their cold creeds.

8
A Legalistic-judgmental Jesus

We can be doctrinaire, not only on theological issues, but on "rules of thumb" as well. Much of life is governed by elaborate sets of rules (mostly shorthand ones) that result from trial and error. They make daily routines much easier: the time we get up in the morning, how to fix our hair, when we eat, etc. In our daily interactions, we quickly learn—"play by the rules." Normally, due to circumstances and when consequences dictate, these rules can be suspended to accommodate change. If the alarm clock fails, I may have to forgo my normal rule about eating if it means missing an important meeting. We do not consider these rules absolute, never to be broken under any circumstance.

When it comes to rules we consider moral or legal, enacted by the church or the state, we tend to hold them more tightly, often out of habit or fear. Some might use their own rigid observance as a club to force compliance or condemn others. The stringent following of rules, no matter what the consequences, is popularly referred to as "legalism" (a term not found in the Bible), shorthand for a sin Jesus implicitly and vigorously condemned and Paul even more so. That's because rules governing religious traditions can be somewhat arbitrary and fickle.

A legalist creates and imposes onerous, unbending rules, or applies existing ones in hardnosed unloving ways. It's like playing golf where the boundaries keep narrowing, so that almost every ball lands out of bounds (how I play golf on a normal course). "Legalism," however, should not be applied to law-gospel/law-grace debates that Christians often use to criticize Jews or Roman Catholics.

A Legalistic-judgmental Jesus

Jesus strongly believes in the law and declares, "Not one letter, not one stroke of a letter will pass from the law until all is accomplished" (Matt 5:18). Legalism emerges in Jesus' Roman occupied world where the more Conservative religious leaders believe God will save Israel if everyone observes very strict purity codes, even those reserved for priests. After all, did not God call the nation to be "a priestly kingdom and a holy nation" (Exod 19:6)? Legalists set very tight restrictions for holy living, irrespective of whether they contribute to or take away from human welfare. When rules harm others, Jesus opposes them for a number of reasons.

First, legalists tend to create an ever growing catalogue of arbitrary rules. In my day, we were given rigid codes that defined the true Christian walk—never drink, smoke, use illegal drugs, dance, engage in premarital sex, use foul language, gamble, play cards, or attend the theater. Generally, these codes stemmed from cultural norms rather than biblical ones. Actually, some rules are beneficial such as censoring smoking, a highly addictive and deadly habit. Yet others, like drinking alcohol, commend moderation, responsibility, and sensitivity. Some, like playing cards, follow from outworn creeds and carry little Christian or *inherent* moral censure. A few, such as dancing and theater-going, are based upon fears of raging sexual arousal, although again responsibility should reign.

Jesus, however, castigates toxic laws, the Corban policy being a case in point. It was selfishly designed to exempt people from financially supporting their aging parents. Here, meanness is veiled by piety's eloquent, "We are giving our money to God." Jesus says this law makes "void the word of God through your tradition that you have handed on" (Mark 7:11–13). Jesus has little patience for the rotting gnarly oaks of arbitrary traditions and their rules that deprive people of happiness and well-being. He never lets up in challenging harmful and oppressive imposed codes, like, as mentioned above, a Sabbath rule that compels people to go hungry.

Second, legalists consider rules as absolute with no exceptions. Truth-telling is a case in point. Immanuel Kant famously argued that one must always tell the truth even if the consequences bring disaster. Any lie chips away at honesty and is ultimately self-defeating, because no one can then be trusted and society will collapse. Even little "white lies," like complimenting someone on their new hairdo when you think it looks hideous, corrodes truth in general.[1]

---

1. Kant, "On the Supposed," 346–50.

Nevertheless, we often admire people who, in extremely trying circumstances, tell a lie for higher purposes such as saving a life. Corrie ten Boom has become a great Christian hero for deceiving the Nazis about hiding Jews in her home. Even the Bible condones life-saving lying when the Pharaoh decrees the death of all Hebrew male babies and instructs the midwives to kill them at birth. They secretly refuse and when male babies start showing up, the midwives tell the Pharaoh a whopper—Hebrew women are built differently and their babies are born before the midwives arrive. God blesses the midwives, even though they lie (Exod 1:15-22). Here, saving lives trumps verbal veracity. However, these are rare exceptions. The truth is always the norm.

Unfortunately, lying is endemic in our society and travels under the names of exaggeration, spin, half-truths, concealing pertinent information, perjury, etc. All the advertising that bombards us daily thrives upon overstatement and misrepresentation. Most skirting of the truth is blatantly self-centered and without moral justification. In chastising those making weaselly oaths or promises, Jesus says, "Whatever you have to say let your 'yes' be a plain 'yes' and your 'no' be a plain 'no'—anything more than that has a taint of evil" (Matt 6:37, Phi). In context Jesus is castigating those who lie for their own gain, which is rarely justified. Exceptions for only the highest moral reasons preserve truth-telling and brings it out from under the glare of legalism.

Third, legalists often major in the minors. Jesus puts it simply and forthrightly, "For you pay your tithe on mint, aniseed, and cumin, and neglect the things which carry far more weight in the Law—justice, mercy, and good faith." This occasions one of his most famous hyperboles, "You filter out the mosquito and swallow the camel" (Matt 23:23-24, Phi). Jesus responds to some legalists who question him about eating without washing, "It is not what goes into the mouth that defiles a person, but what . . . proceeds from the heart—evil intentions, murder, adultery, fornication, theft, false witness, slander. These are what defile a person, but to eat with unwashed hands does not defile" (Matt 15: 11-20). Here, Jesus critiques legalistic nit-picking in lieu of the more compelling Ten Commandments and social justice. Thus, one could feel quite smug in keeping a strict sexual code against obscenity, yet manifest little civic conscience regarding the putrid obscenities of bigotry, of corporate marauding, or of the military invasion of other countries. Moreover, conspicuously absent from the legalist's concerns are the personal rules designed to save life and Planet such as: don't eat junk food, exercise daily, don't invest in or buy products that exploit foreign labor and/or harm the environment, etc.

Fourth, legalists tend to look at the letter of the law rather than its inner spirit. For Jesus, one must major in love, the highest value from which all rules must "hang" (or are interpreted by [Matt 22:39–40]). This means every law or rule, must pass the love God/love neighbor-enemy test. Thus, Jesus rejects the "eye for an eye" law of retaliation in favor of "do not resist the evildoer," "turn the other cheek," "go the second mile," "give to everyone who begs from you," and "do not refuse anyone who wants to borrow from you" (Matt 5:38–42). *Lex talionis* legalists find these acts of love incomprehensible if not nauseous.

Fifth, Jesus also opposes legalism because of its seductive bed partner—judgmentalism. The Judgmental Jesus swims in an ocean filled with petty rules used to censor others, like the Jim Crow laws directed against minorities. Certainly, being held accountable for wrongdoing undergirds all community building. Judgmentalism, however, seeps in when we search out, magnify, and condemn in others what our overly strict and often arbitrary rules prohibit. Judgmentalism lurks deep within us all and is quick to surface. By assuming a "holier than thou" attitude, even on very minor issues, we can hide our own macro-moral failures.

In truth, most of us probably feel slight glee in the pitfalls of others, especially for those we happen not to like. However, delivering harsh and censoring moral judgments reflects the insidious vice of pride—thinking ourselves better than others amidst our own moral failings. Those quick to judge believe they are preserving faith's purity and, consequently, are walking much closer to Jesus. Actually, judgmental religious leaders who secretly violate their own strict rules, give Jesus fodder to condemn hypocrisy. Hypocrites "devour widows' houses" and "clean the outside of the cup and of the plate, but inside they are full of greed and self-indulgence." (Mark 12:40; See Matt 23 for a whole litany of hypocrisy's sins). Yet, we all must admit that we are practicing hypocrites to some degree.

Because we all live in fragile glass houses, we must constantly guard against casting stones. Jesus directly addresses this quandary: "Let the one among you who has never sinned throw the first stone at her" and "take the log out of your own eye, and then you can see clearly to take the speck out of your neighbor's eye" (John 8:7 Phi; Matt 7:5). He summarizes, "Do not judge so that you may not be judged" (Matt 7:1). Jesus forthrightly condemns judgmentalism because it perpetuates distancing in the human community. From its perceived superiority, judgmentalism lacks forgiveness, humility, and the empathy to identify with others as pilgrims, struggling along life's journeys with all its pitfalls. Leaden legalism with its judgmental toxin insidiously poisons our moral character.

Furthermore, judging others blinds us from seeing how people, including ourselves, are victimized by flawed ethical/legal systems, inadequate knowledge, media propaganda, overzealous Christians, strong-arming religious leaders, past abuses, or horrendous social conditions like discrimination, toxic cultural traditions, rigid class structures, and economic disparities. That is why Jesus says from the cross, "Father forgive them, for they do not know what they are doing" (Luke 23:34). Jesus exonerates his executioners because they are victims of an imperial legalistic/judgmental system. Jesus relentlessly opposes legalism and its vices, while showing awe-inspiring compassion to those victimized by them. Likewise, we too must be overly cautious to avoid legalism and its attending judgmentalism. When smitten with them, we languish in vainglory that demolishes character and belittles the humble non-judgmental Jesus.

9
A Positive-thinking Jesus

Americans have been inundated with countless self-help schemes alleging to improve their standing, financial prowess, physical and mental health, sexual performance, and on and on. One claim is that the road to success entails substituting negative thoughts for positive ones. Tough times torment us because of our weak mental and spiritual attitude—our capitulation to the flow of events. A Christianized version suggests that positive thoughts can overcome our trials and temptations and pave the road to victorious Christian living. The Positive Thinking Gospel is closely tied to the Prosperity Gospel. God wants us to be successful in every way—have a better house and reward us with health, wealth, and happiness. What normally follows are a host of "formulas for success" such as repeating, "I can do great things." Of course, "I" is the primary focal point.

Its original and most popular guru was Norman Vincent Peale with his "Power of Positive Thinking" movement. Later, Robert Schuller would don Peale's mantle under the rubric of "Possibility Thinking." More recently this approach has been popularized by Joel Osteen, who has elevated positive thinking to new heights. He encourages Christians to rid themselves of a "defeatist mentality" and call upon God, not just for favor, but "heavy favor." This means "think big" and "pray big" when all odds are against you. Then God "will do something you have never seen." Osteen sprinkles his sermons with high-flown anecdotes like the man who asked shoe manufacturers to donate 3,000 shoes for children in Africa, only to have one company commit a million pair. This story's real power; however, is not in thinking big, but in its generosity toward the poor.

In this approach, the purpose of Jesus is to help us think better about ourselves and look upon our difficulties more positively. Then, our dreams of victory and abundance will come true. This view seizes upon Jesus' command "to love your neighbor as yourself," but considers the "as yourself" to be an added command—you must love yourself first. So the goal of faith is to discover our lost self-esteem, making it easier to change our perspectives and overcome plaguing circumstances.

Thinking positively is certainly beneficial for the mind, for others, and for our world. In many situations we probably should see the glass half full rather than half empty. Also, thinking positively about one's self is a worthy psychological goal, playing an important role in maturation and productivity. The Reverend Jessie Jackson uses positive thinking to help instill dignity to youth within the inner cities. Unfortunately, the Positive Thinking movement assumes that human beings have total control over their lives. The ethos of individualism that flows through the veins of America's character feeds it. It undergirds America's "lift yourself up by your own bootstraps" mentality, supposing one's predicament is caused by mental failure, often implied as moral failure. The individualism that underlies this theology has merit; but when overdone, it fails to grasp the complexities of life and diminishes the role that social, economic, and political factors constantly play in a person's tribulations and achievements.

When one's esteem or dignity is assaulted daily because of childhood abuse, abject poverty, degrading bigotry, or political oppression, it remains difficult for that person to find any power in positive thinking or retain feelings of self-worth. Much suffering throughout history is due to cultural codes and circumstances over which the majority of people exercise little control. The unknown billions of destitute on Earth will never receive "heavy favor," but face heavy hunger and heavy misery daily. Their only hope is obtaining something meager just to survive. Today hundreds of children starve as I write this paragraph and any exhortation for attitude change or self-reliance will seem but a cruel hoax. While the gospel of self-reliance may have some relevance in an affluent society with opportunities, even then, peoples' prospects are largely conditioned by their social and economic circumstances. Opportunities are not universal, especially for minorities.[1] Yes, Jesus says, "with God all things are possible," but this

---

1. See the National Urban League's, *The State of Black America*. Key findings are that Black household wealth is only 6 cents for every white dollar. Hispanics are not much better at 7 cents. Unemployment among Blacks is twice that of Whites.

phrase was uttered in the context of a rich ruler who, because of wealth's powerful pull, refused to help the poor (Matt 19:26). For him, like many of us with defiant wills, God's possibilities are never realized.

Overemphasizing positive thinking paints a distorted picture of Jesus, especially when it ignores the more important dimensions of his mission. Jesus' inaugural speech challenges the "heavy favor" that his hometown friends and family are expecting God to shower upon them. In fact, Jesus implies that God intentionally *disfavors* them by passing them over. Because Jesus rejects their Osteenian theology, the enraged townsfolk try to kill him (Luke 4:16–30). A person of character addresses not only the possibilities in life, but also its challenges.

Jesus offers no individual "bootstraps" advice to peasants under the imperial order, except to enter into a Kingdom of mutual cooperation with its loving laws and policies. Only such a community will reverse their negative conditions. Furthermore, this Kingdom repudiates the prevailing honor/shame codes and will restore self-esteem as "those who humble themselves will be exalted" (Luke 14:11). The truly honorable or "respectable" person; however, is the "one who serves others" (Matt 23:11, Phi). The *genuine* positive thinker thinks of positive ways to consider the interests of others, mirroring the mind and character of Christ and of Paul.

We are to strive, but "strive first for the Kingdom of God and its justice . . ." (Matt 6:33). Here Jesus admonishes us to think more positively and work more vigorously for the type of governing that assures social and economic justice. Otherwise, the Positive-Thinking Gospel masquerades as self-righteousness and ignores Jesus' broader mission, disrespects him, and does him no favor.

10
An Anti-intellectual Jesus

One of the more pervasive and frightening misunderstandings of Jesus links him to irrationality and anti-intellectualism. Throughout the centuries, Christians have been known to disregard facts, truth, science, statistics, and logic in making claims about their beliefs. In fact, some Christians express contempt for science and reason and consider ignorance almost a virtue, giving rise to the witticism, "I have made up my mind, don't confuse me with the facts."

The problem for us is that the Bible was written in a prescientific age governed by "what you see is what you get." The scientific method deals with discoveries that often run counter to what we see, such as a flat, stationary Earth, around which the sun revolves. Like those living in biblical times, and even today, we would have no way of knowing that these are "naïve beliefs," if not for the work of scientists. Unfortunately, many Christians have declared a "war on science" in favor of their reading of Scripture, filtering out any peer-reviewed evidence that challenges their renderings.[1] However, like any tool, reason and science can serve both good and evil.

Soren Kierkegaard, who had a great impact upon contemporary theology, challenged the extreme rationalism that had permeated eighteenth century theology. Pitting faith against reason, he argued that something irrational, like the death of Christ bringing salvation, takes more faith to believe. While some think his theology promotes *irrationalism*, a more sympathetic interpretation is that he wanted to highlight the *nonrational* within Christianity. After all, his voluminous writings are cogently argued

1. Achenbauch, "The Age," 40.

and make a lot of sense; they are not unreasonable. Yet, irrational ideas, illogical arguments, and contempt of science continue as a legacy within the Christian Church.

Wisdom has always played a significant role in the Judeo-Christian faith. A large segment of the Hebrew Scripture is labeled "Wisdom," including books like Proverbs, Ecclesiastes, and Job. Throughout these books, the wise person is contrasted with the fool. Ultimately, the folly of fools distances them from God: "Fools say in their hearts, 'There is no God.'" Foolishness is followed by moral failure: "They are corrupt, they do abominable deeds; there is no one who does good" (Ps 14:1). Thus, the fool not only acts stupidly and unspiritually, but also heartlessly. Foolishness, then, inhibits character building. This moral truth underlies Jesus' parable about a rich man who built huge barns to hoard his grain, while the masses starved. God calls him a "fool" because of his "greed," and his belief that life "consists in the abundance of possessions" (Luke 12:13–21).

Jesus summarizes his passion for truth when he says, "I am the way, and the truth, and the life" (John 14:6). While reason and facts do not define faith, they are surely essential ingredients of it. So important was wisdom for Jesus that when he quotes the greatest command about loving God "with all your heart, soul, and strength," he adds, "with all your mind." I often warned my students that a cavalier attitude toward study and knowledge reflects upon our love and devotion to God. When a scribe says that this great command is more important than all the burnt offerings and sacrifices, Jesus confirms his "wise" response (Mark 12:30–34).

Jesus' famous Golden Rule is grounded in one of Aristotle's rules of reason, the principle of non-contradiction—treating like things alike. Paul wants love to "overflow" with "knowledge and full insight" so people may do what is "best" (Phil 1:9, Phi). A later epistle exhorts believers to give reasons for their faith (1 Pet 3:15). Given his emphasis upon wisdom, Jesus was later memorialized by John as the "logos" or the first principle of philosophy and by Paul as the "wisdom of God" (John 1:1; 1 Cor 1:24, 30). To possess Christ's mind is to possess a wise mind and why a person of character acts intelligently.

Since the Garden of Pride, we all tend not to admit when we are wrong. We expertly devise strategies to protect cherished beliefs and to save face, becoming masters of half-truths, spins, selective facts, and distortions. We also learn how to violate the formal and informal rules of logic with ease. I remember the "guilt by association" heaped upon Billy Graham because he shared the stage with Norman Vincent Peale at some ecumenical event; or the "ad hominem" (attacking a person rather than their ideas) to discredit Martin Luther King, Jr. by alleging he was a communist.

Self-interest plays a large part in how one perceives reality and whether one will be a "truth denier." For years tobacco companies publically denied the deadly effects of smoking in the face of overwhelming scientific evidence. Similarly, Exxon/Mobil publically questions human-induced climate change while internally constructing its business model on the reality of such change. Paralleling the evolution debate, a few "extractive states" (where coal and oil are major economic drivers) have introduced school curriculum that counters climate change science. Some Christians follow suit and stand at the forefront of the climate denier movement, although many believers affirm Creation-care and work hard to preserve God's beautiful Planet.

The Anti-intellectual Jesus leads to the most bizarre beliefs. For instance, in a Gallup poll, 67 percent of American Christians look at Genesis quite literally and believe that Earth and human beings were created by God only 6,000 years ago, as Bishop James Ussher calculated.[2] This literal understanding of Genesis flies in the face of facts in virtually all scientific fields such as astronomy, cosmology, paleontology, molecular biology, archeology, and climatology. It even disparages the fundamental principles of physics, mathematics, and chemistry, the basic building blocks of all significant advancements in contemporary life. While scientists may disagree on many details about dating and origins, virtually all consider that Earth is billions of years old and human beings have been around for hundreds of thousands of years. The young Earth belief leads to absurd conclusions: that humans and dinosaurs lived together; that all the geologic layers are a result of Noah's forty day flood; that all the deep canyons like the Grand Canyon were carved by receding flood waters; that fossils take only a few years to form; and that carbon and other isotope datings are completely off base. To hold the whole scientific enterprise in contempt is a breathtaking assault upon the truth and upon the one who is The Truth.

Take Flood Geology. It is totally discredited today, although its defenders appear regularly on the church channels. When one contemplates God's awesome laws of Nature, the mighty forces of wind, rain, and erosion behind the Colorado River carving out the Grand Canyon over a four million year period, it staggers the mind. In addition, a hundred million years of

---

2. Gallup, hold-creationist-view-human-origin.aspx

sediments deposited by oceans covering and receding and animals becoming fossilized, along with forces lifting the plateau from which the Canyon was formed, only add to our amazement and wonder. These mighty works of God over vast stretches of times are, unfortunately, never appreciated by those who believe in an instantly created Earth. Beauty lies, not only in the end product, but also in the wondrous complex forces that create and shape our Planet . . . and why we enjoy watching great artists at work.

God must grieve at the crude disrespect for the majestic laws that God built into Nature. Is not slighting God's natural laws as grave as slighting God's moral laws? Do we not sully divine truth by believing God deliberately deceives us into thinking Earth is old when it is not? These views make God small and also diminish the majesty of Jesus through whom this Universe lives, moves, and has its being.

Anti-intellectualism, however, can have more than just unfortunate consequences. It could also lead to dangerous, even disastrous results. In his famous sermon Jesus speaks of a "foolish man who built his house upon the sand. The rain fell, and the floods came, and the winds blew and beat against the house and it fell—and great was its fall" (Matt 7:26–27). Note that Jesus calls the man who ignores the science behind the forces of Nature and the physics of house construction a "fool." The lack of a critical rational mindset has led many duped people to foolishly invest in bogus get-rich-quick schemes that have stripped away their life savings. Some scorn proven medical science such as common immunizations, exposing their children and others to controllable diseases.

On a grand scale, misinformation and irrational fear can even drive nations to readily engage in war and unimaginable slaughter. Ignoring the science of global climate change could put billions of people in jeopardy from polluted air, rising and acidic oceans, melting glaciers, arable land succumbing to encroaching desert, and more. When Christians lend the voice of Jesus to their disregard of factual evidence or to irrational notions, they not only jeopardize the future of Earth and its inhabitants, but also belittle the Jesus of truth. This lack of critical thinking stifles growth in character and often leads to another way Jesus is made small—to magical thinking.

11
A Magical-thinking Jesus

Have you ever attended a ballgame when, with only a few seconds left, the losing team must pull off a perfect winning play? While the fans are holding their breath, they also hold their hands together in prayer for God's miraculous intervention. In football, that last long desperation pass into the end zone has been christened a "hail Mary," hoping that somehow Jesus' mother will intercede for a long shot touchdown. For luck, some coaches wear the same sports jacket each game. All these are based upon superstition and they prevail everywhere in daily life, from black cats crossing our paths to walking under ladders.

When a sports team happens to win, some point a finger and look toward heaven. This assumes that the losing team is bereft of God's favor. Actually, such a view is a form of idolatry, since it denies the true God for a lesser god, one who chooses sides. While the outcome of football games is relatively innocent, when God is heralded to take sides, let's say, in war, the effects are catastrophic.

Magical thinking is a normal part of childhood, encouraged and reinforced by fairy tales and beliefs in Santa Claus, the Tooth Fairy, and the Easter Bunny. As a child, when on a family vacation to California, I saw a group of children riding a miniature train in someone's front yard. I was completely enthralled by it. For the remainder of the trip I desperately ached that a similar train appear in my own front yard. I believed if I prayed hard enough, God would provide it. And so I prayed and prayed long, silently, and expectantly—the whole trip. I believed beyond any doubt that a shining engine, a row of painted cars, and a winding track would greet me in my front yard. As we pulled up to our house, I looked out the window,

A Magical-thinking Jesus

and saw only a bare, overgrown, weed-infested lawn. I was crushed. As you now know, I've never erased the disappointment.

One might think that as we grow older and live in an age where the scientific method affects nearly everything we do, a belief in magic would hold little sway. Yet, one of the most read parts of a daily newspaper is the astrology section, which thrives on magical thinking—that the motion of distant stars could somehow influence one's personal circumstances in significant ways. Reading fortune cookies at Chinese restaurants can be entertaining, but does anyone believe they possess predictive power?

Magical thinking Christians shrink at the idea of random activity, coincidences, or chance. Since God controls every event, the only way to change something is to cajole God into making the change we wish. Of course, strict Calvinists believe that the most mundane event is predetermined and controlled by God, so all the prayer in the world changes nothing. For others, if something does happen by coincidence, they might consider it a miracle of God.

Christians, however, do not hold a monopoly on depicting an event as divine intervention. Karma, Kabbalah, prayer wheels, rosaries, incense, voodoo, and rituals are all grounded in magical thinking and suppress credible views of cause and effect. Yet, the more we know about the workings of the Universe and its physical laws, even in producing a blade of grass, the more we are awestruck by Creation's integrity and beauty—and complexity. We need to be careful not to attribute miracles to our knowledge gap of Creation's intricate physical laws.

Magical thinking actually holds God's physical laws in contempt. We should not expect Jesus to wave a magic wand and violate laws of Nature whenever any difficulty blows our way. Despite the reassuring claims of some preachers, not every illness is cured; not every problem is solved no matter how much we pray and how much we believe. Moreover, God's moral laws and our moral character languish due to the deception, arrogance, and greed that underwrite the constant bombardment of magical thinking around us.

Prosperity preachers effectively use magical thinking to exploit people, promising special miracles for those who donate to their cause. Anointed handkerchiefs, miracle spring water, and special prayer blankets ($27.50 + shipping) guarantee powers for healing and financial success. When the gullible—out of a trust in these good luck charms—shun well-established financial plans or medical cures, the results could be disastrous. A houseless

PART 1—BELITTLING JESUS

man, one of the victims of an Orange County, CA serial killer, was warned by police to go to a shelter and not sleep alone. His response: "I feel like God will take care of me—it's all in God's hands." Magical thinking trumped his considering a safe alternative and cost him his life.[1] Such thinking also serves to reinforce social prejudices like the religious leaders who attribute a natural disaster to divine punishment for tolerating homosexuality.

The magical approach also hits home in claims like, "The Lord spoke to me," or "The Lord told me," as if someone possessed a direct pipeline to the divine. Such talk betrays subtle pride by promoting one's ideas and outlooks as buttressed by divine authority. In my sixty years as an Evangelical Christian, I have never once heard the unmediated voice of God. I'm cautious here, though, since my theology—that revelation comes indirectly, but primarily through the Word—precludes divine earphones. Unfortunately, it is nearly impossible to debate those who believe God speaks to them privately, no matter how unusual or even foolish their utterances seem. Televangelists talk incessantly about their direct communications with God.

Hundreds of superstitions and mythologies have plagued and/or governed human societies for centuries. Most of us succumb to magical thinking in some way. It remains so pervasive that nearly every commercial assumes that people will believe even the most exaggerated claims: this exercise device will create the perfect physique; this cream will rid every wrinkle; and read this book and make millions. It gives rise to the joke that the difference between a church and a casino is that when you pray in a casino, you really mean it. Can one's prayers really affect the roll of the dice or the button on a slot machine? Speaking of prayer, is it a form of magical thinking? "Keep me in your prayers" is a common Christian request. Do prayers make a difference?

Some years ago a famous study claimed that "distant" intercessory prayers helped heart patients improve. Later and larger studies could not replicate the findings, and now the earlier study is considered flawed.[2] Whether prayer is effective or not depends on how one views its meaning and significance. If one considers prayer as a manipulative technique that badgers God to change events, then prayer is reduced to magical thinking. Rather, as Mother Teresa said, "Prayer is not asking. Prayer is putting oneself in the hands of God . . ." It verbalizes gratitude to the Power beyond

---

1. Branson-Potts, et al., "Ocampo 'wasn't done,'" A1, A8.
2. See Cadge, "Saying Your Prayers," 299–327.

A Magical-thinking Jesus

us, while expressing our concerns into words to discern God's will and act accordingly.

What about Jesus' exhortation to "ask and it shall be given you?" Does this mean God answers every prayer? Jesus assures us that the Heavenly Parent only "gives good gifts." God does not answer prayers that *we might think* are good, but turn out to be "stones" or "snakes" (Matt 7:7–11). In a parallel account Jesus says, "The heavenly Father will give the Holy Spirit to those who ask him," a strange substitute for the "good gifts" people normally expect when asking God for something (Luke 11:9–13). Why would God give the Holy Spirit?

The Holy Spirit is given because the Spirit is power. Prayer is an act of empowerment during times our character needs strengthening. The Spirit also gifts people with special skills and instills "love, joy, peace, patience, kindness, generosity, faithfulness, gentleness and self-control," the "fruit" or character traits that contribute to answered prayer (Rom 12:6–8; Gal 5:22–23). As someone once said, "Prayer doesn't always change things, but changes people who change things." The Spirit also intercedes for us, because in "our weakness, we do not know how to pray as we ought"—the reason some prayers are not answered (Rom 8:26, with Jas 4:3). The "weakness" here is our selfish mindset, reinforced by ingrained cultural values, blinding us to God's will and leaving us in desperate need of the Spirit's power and intercession. The Spirit helps expose the spirit-quenching hidden forces that affect our daily journey. Thus, every prayer must be bathed in the humility of Jesus' prayer, "Not my will, but yours be done" (Luke 22:42).

Much of what Jesus says about prayer criticizes its misuse, especially prayers that prey. He castigates those who "stand and pray in the synagogues and street corners, so that they may be seen of others." Here he bemoans the showy public prayers, like those offered today in local city councils or schools (functions of the synagogue in his day). Rather, "pray to your Father who is in secret." Nor does he wish believers to "heap up empty phrases," thinking "they will be heard because of their many words." Prayers that are repetitious, are too lengthy, or overly fancy go no further than the sound of one's voice, and, as God says in Isaiah, "Even though you make many prayers, I will not listen" (Isa 1:15). Furthermore, he frowns upon prayers that keep informing God what we need, because "your Father knows what you need before you ask him" (Matt 6:5–8). Jesus' points are that we can blaspheme God, even while in prayer.

Jesus' own deeply passionate prayer request in the Garden of Gethsemane begins with, "If it is possible, let this cup pass from me" (Matt 26:39, 42). By ending it with, "your will be done." Jesus does not assume an expected answer, but focuses upon God's will, as found in *Scripture*. For Jesus, prayer means getting in touch with God's will, accepting it, and acting upon it with humility and power. Manipulating God for some magical deliverance is absent in his prayer. Let us learn from Jesus and pray in the spirit of "if it is possible," and always bow before God's will. Then our prayers are more authentic, more Christ-like, and more life and world changing.

Jesus provides us with a model prayer we call The Lord's Prayer (Matt 6:9–11). It takes only fifteen seconds to pray (preachers, take note), is communal ("our" and "us" sprinkled throughout the prayer), and focuses upon Jesus' biggest concern—"your kingdom come, your will be done, on Earth . . . ." Notice again the emphasis upon God's will and that it "be done" or acted upon. What's to be done is to establish a whole new political order (God's Kingdom), not a trivial matter. This new governing provides the necessary ingredients for human survival as articulated in the prayer ("daily bread," Land "debt forgiveness," and fair court "trials"). These petitions make the Prayer universal and relevant now for the billions who wage the daily war on want, falling through torn safety nets; *and for us who have the means to answer their prayers*. That's its "magical" power and also a warning—that, for instance, when we pray for God to end hunger, we will participate in answering that prayer and not berate government for its part in doing so.

Actually, a great contribution of the Judeo-Christian faith is that it vigorously opposed the realm of magic that governed ancient societies, breaking its stranglehold and control. When Jesus attacks ritual performances, purity and dining codes, nit-picking Sabbath laws, long rambling and vain repetitious prayers, and the rigid honor system, he undercuts the magical thinking upon which these practices were based. Jesus assumes a cause/effect universe. For instance, when he claims that God feeds the birds of the air, he is not suggesting that birds sit in their nests and wait for worms to "miraculously" fall out of the sky. Rather, they leave the nest and forage. This is the miracle of nature that surrounds us. As Bev Shea used to sing, "I've seen a lily push its way up through the stubborn sod, I believe in miracles, for I believe in God." Jesus' God is the all-powerful force of Nature whose will operates, not only through moral and legal laws, but also through natural laws that create lilies.

A Magical-thinking Jesus

    The old cliché that "God helps those who help themselves," while overly individualistic, at least counters the passive hope for God's blessings to magically appear. To make Jesus into someone who encourages passivity or laziness undercuts rational action. To engage in magical thinking is yet another way we make Jesus small and dismantle moral character. The Magical-thinking Jesus also reinforces other distortions of Jesus such as believing he can solve all our problems, fix everything broken, and lift us out of every predicament, to which we now turn.

12

A Problem-solving Jesus

Some Christians construe Jesus as a grand problem-solver. Whatever the issue, he will provide a ready-made answer. While Jesus does provide solutions to many of life's problems, like fixing broken relationships and social structures, he does not provide answers to everything that plagues us. For instance, I once dreamed of building my own house, but such an effort seemed far beyond my abilities. Then, I read some home construction books and I am now living in my fifth owner-built house. Although Jesus was a tradesperson, he did not teach me much about home construction and the many technical problems I faced (except the foolishness of building a house upon sand). I needed to know the physics of forces and shears placed upon building materials so they safely withstand weight, earthquake, fire, or fierce winds. Jesus might give me the good sense to hire a licensed engineer, but he would not provide me a set of drawings and calculations.

Because humans are fashioned in the image of God, the Creator, we are also naturally creative. Jesus did instill character traits needed to build a house, such as patience, courage, tenacity, calmness, and honesty—virtues necessary to succeed in any field. However, these qualities are not substitutes for a competence that is beyond the scope of Jesus' instruction. *Jesus came primarily to solve one problem, the problem of individual and corporate sin and its effects.* Looking to him for detailed instructions on every subject is to warp his mission.

Yet, some see Jesus solving problems in arenas he never intended to address, such as providing a model for running a successful business.[1] Jesus

---

1. Zabloski, *The 25 Most Common*, 5–262.

A Problem-solving Jesus

is a visionary, a risk-taker, diligent, and never cheats anyone—necessary ingredients for all endeavors. However, Jesus wishes to model what it takes to enter the Kingdom. His vision for CEO's would be to sell the business and give the proceeds to the poor or at least share the profits with them. For Jesus, risk-taking means taking risks in the face of injustice. He has no interest in providing guidance to make smart business decisions (like whether to start a video store in the Netflix era). Here one's vision must be buttressed by sensible marketing strategy and financial planning. We belittle Jesus when we ask him to solve such problems.

Jesus does teach us to be fair and honest in all our dealings and not deceive people with spins, exaggerations, fine print, or leaving important information unsaid. This may mean only a 10 percent markup on a product rather than gouging people, as hotels do on weekends. Jesus expects a used car dealer to diligently learn about each car and expose everything about that car to a prospective buyer. Furthermore, if we were as moral as Jesus requires, we might not engage in some business endeavors like coal extraction, raising beef, and manufacturing plastic bags. Another question Christians tend to ignore is: would Jesus ever approve of an economy based upon unrestrained capitalism?

Some predicaments are beyond our control (explored in the next chapter), but many are self-inflicted, resulting from foolish choices. Praying before an exam is not a substitute for lack of study nor is prayer a bailout due to poor budgeting or foolish spending. Yet, God does not give up on us. Jesus tells a story about a prodigal son who, lacking good character, makes some bad choices and ends up disgraced (Luke 15:11–32). Moreover, the son's father (representing God) does not chase after his son and badger him about wasting his money on wine and women. Even when the son becomes desperate, the father does not intervene to bail him out of the pig pen. Yet, the father remains present in the son's memory, allowing him to "come to his senses." The son finally makes a good "common sense" decision (better off at home than here), comes home, apologizes, and lives a productive life. The father, without judgment, without conditions, welcomes him back with open arms. The moral: God never abandons us, but give us the common sense to work through our desperate problems and, hopefully, make the wise and character-grounded decisions.

As noted above, the ethos of this age is to gain more and more, even though Jesus warns us that "life does not consist in the abundance of possessions" or "what will it profit them to gain the whole world and forfeit

PART 1—BELITTLING JESUS

their life?" (Luke 12:15; Mark 8:32). Yet, our unchecked lure for anything and everything often morphs into bad habits and leaves us wallowing in a myriad of problems. What we drink, smoke, eat, buy, and other lifestyle decisions may contribute to strokes, heart attacks, cancers, and other ailments. Like the prodigal son, we can be left mentally, physically, socially, economically, morally, and spiritually bankrupt. We hit bottom. However, God has created us with the sense to search for solutions, both in ourselves and with the support of others. Jesus' role is to remain in our memory with love and hope, await the return to our senses, welcome us with open arms, and empower us to his better place in life.

Although Jesus can provide strength of character that includes love, patience, and all the other fruit of the Spirit to cope with disasters, he does not directly intervene to right all wrongs or solve every problem we create. To rely on Jesus for something he expects from us is yet another way we discredit him and his role in how we deal with self-imposed problems. But what about evils that hit us "out of the blue?"

13
A Quick-fix Jesus

Most of us have been victimized by misfortunes—events beyond our control. Many are plagued by disease and some suffer at the hands of vicious persons and unjust institutions that foster racism, poverty, genderism, etc. The problems of pain, bad outcomes, and evil in the world are vexing. Why would an omnipotent, all-wise, and all-loving God permit misfortune and suffering? Yet, let's not be too quick to impugn God.

First, biologically, pain is a built-in warning system of danger and essential for human and animal survival, and thus, ironically, a gift from the all-caring God. Second, we should also acknowledge that some or even much of the pain and suffering in this world is human-induced and a result of misshapen social and political forces. Many cancers feed on chemical toxins introduced into our atmosphere and water through human activities. We call them "diseases of civilization." Consider the unimaginable atrocities of war and the everyday violence around us. Is God to blame? God desires a peaceful paradise, but humans choose otherwise.

In reality, we are all traveling a path that ultimately leads to death. The way is littered with misfortune and accident, constants of human life that guarantee a "Murphy's Law world." For some, daily adversities are trivial yet annoying, such as misplacing keys, stubbing a toe, or knocking over a water glass, although any one may become a breaking point. Catastrophic events, like the loss of a job, the foreclosure of a home, a divorce, or the death of a loved one, bring devastation. For many, especially minorities or the houseless, life may be unbearably wretched due to personal and structural prejudice and its continuing torment.

During a difficult time, some well-intended friend might say, "Think of all the good things Jesus has done for you." This counsel is like the doctor, who, after discovering a deadly melanoma, tells the patient, "Oh! Don't fret over this little cancer; the rest of your body is just fine." Given the gravity of melanoma, few patients would find comfort in such advice. While it remains true that Jesus has met past needs and could help us deal with misfortune, he never guarantees smooth sailing or wants us to live in denial.

Some others might advise, "Just trust him more." While having more trust is always good counsel, it too, does not guarantee a quick fix. Indeed, to trust in a Fix-all Jesus and its fatalistic and dismissive corollaries is ironically a gigantic *failure* of faith—the lack of faith that God has created humans with the strength and ability to face tragedy, look for solutions, seek help, and not expect Jesus to make everything right. Some might resign themselves to tragedy as "the Lord's will." This Christian fatalism could distract us from an obvious remedy. Moreover, resignation could trigger a downward spiral into the deeper morass of alcohol, drugs, or ultimately, suicide. As the model for comfort and hope, we look to Jesus, not to fix what goes wrong, but to share our grief and hear his promise that "I am with you always" (Matt 28:20).

Some might chalk up misfortune to "learning experiences"—Lucy's answer to Charlie Brown after losing every football game by lopsided scores. His response: "Then I must be the smartest person in the world." Certainly coping with disaster can be beneficial; and our faith in and closeness to Jesus plays a significant role. But just as Jesus is not a problem solver, so we should not expect him to undo all our misfortunes. Furthermore, considering Jesus a cosmic handyman subjects him to blame for not ending our troubles. The important point is not whether Jesus puts all the pieces back together from life's brokenness, but rather *how* Jesus helps us to deal with the embers of hell that blow our way; how he constructs the path of character, boring through the mountains we face. What is the role of Jesus in a ruinous world?

First, Christians should never think that Jesus has promised a life immune from suffering. Indeed, he assures, "Favored are those who are persecuted for justice' sake" (Matt 5:10). Paul backs this up with "God has graciously granted you the privilege . . . to suffer for him" (Phil 1:29). Few of us would think of suffering as a privilege or a gift of grace. While no Christian should masochistically search out suffering, yet when it comes, we confront it and struggle with it. The devastating misfortunes, such as the death of a loved one, are fraught with psychological dangers like depression, fear, debilitating sorrow, as well as social and economic setbacks. For some, there will never be a light at the end of the tunnel. They remain in a dark labyrinth where they see only a flicker of light here and there. Jesus provides not only glimmers of comforting endurance to make the night not so forlorn, but also grants us the courage to face what's broken and, if possible, for us to fix it.

Second, Jesus' goal is to bring about God's promised way of governing to his people engulfed in imperial evils. He names this governing the "Kingdom of God" and it will bring deliverance from civilization's cruel, exploitive, and violent story of the few persecuting the vast majority. Consider all the slaughtering, torturing, and holocausts throughout history due to regional fighting and world wars. True, humans are classified as animals, but are not tied to instinct alone. God gifts us with a will to choose between good and evil. Yet, our will may not be as free as we think. The fear/fight/flight instinct, embedded within the human brain, yields a culture of self-preservation, bigotry, and violence that worms its way into all our institutions. Like Cain, we choose to slay our kin and, with spurious justifications, do so with relative ease and a clear conscience. This is why Jesus tells us to pray for the Kingdom to come on Earth—so that *God's will* might be done.

Jesus is especially concerned about the evils done to those labeled "sinners"—those who ignore the strict codes of the pious cultural warriors. He "welcomes sinners and eats with them," providing us a model for dealing with cultural devilry (Luke 15:2). On a broader scale, Jesus sees the answer to wrongdoing when bad governing is replaced by a safety net governing that assures free health care and free food, welcomes strangers/immigrants, clothes the unclothed, provides clean drinking water, and affirms the dignity of prisoners (Matt 11:5, 25:35–45). As that form of governing dawns, our broken world can heal. We must partner with Jesus to make it happen (by voting for it) and encourage people to "enter" it.

Thus, when facing broader community evils, Christians are not to remain passive, but rather "strive" for "justice" (Matt 6:33). Christians bring Jesus' Kingdom values to the social, economic, and ecological table, becoming a part of community problem solving that rights the wrongs of people, institutions, and nations. As someone once said, if we ask God, "Why do you allow these evils to happen?," God will direct the question right back to us.

PART 1—BELITTLING JESUS

Yet, did not Jesus perform miracles to get people out of jams? Once, at a wedding, he saves the party and the host's reputation by turning water into the most exquisite wine. He also performs healing miracles, bringing wholeness to many. Do such miracles still happen today? Watching all the faith healers on the church channels, one might think so. However, we must exercise extreme caution with the following observations.

First, in fairness it must be said that some people are genuinely helped by faith healers. Because some illnesses are psychosomatic (mind induced), our mental state can play a significant role in our health. Possibly, some on-stage-healings are of this nature. Second, we never observe external healings like withered limbs immediately growing to normal size (a healing that Jesus performed), although Pentecostals carry a bag full of oral anecdotes of such happenings. I have watched many performance "healings" on TV and all have been internal and nonobservable.

Third, as mentioned before, many of the faith healers are showmen. Like frontier snake-oil charlatans (the oils are now packaged as "anointing oils"), they prey upon the misfortunes of people. Their appeals often guarantee results as they beg for donations, the usual precondition for God's promised healing blessing. Christianity, though, is not unique in promoting miraculous healings. In one Eastern tradition, many believe that a famous Guru, whose arm fell off, simply picked it up and attached it back like new. To believe such things assumes extreme gullibility.

Fourth, even though Jesus performs miracles, he never wants to be labeled a miracle worker. In fact, he avoids healing shows. After his healing fame in Capernaum had spread and he returns to his hometown, the people jam the synagogue hoping to witness a healing. He refuses to perform, but rather delivers a *prophetic critique*, prefacing it with "no prophet is accepted in the prophet's hometown." He then recalls past healings by the prophets Elijah and Elisha and, with some interpretative license, points out that they healed *non-Israelites*. As we have seen, this riled the congregation (Luke 4:16–30).

This inaugural event presages his later healings. He downplays the miraculous dimension in favor of their prophetic purpose—as signs of the promised new governing with its inclusive health care and the religious/political intrigue and controversy that surrounds such governing (Matt 10:7–8). Thus, he gets in trouble because he heals on the Sabbath, forgives the sins of the sick, and heals women, Gentiles, Samaritans, the blind, and those with skin diseases—all of whom were shunned due to religio-political restrictions.

The same holds true for Jesus' exorcisms. The exorcism of Legion (obliquely referring to Rome's Legions), who resides in the graveyard of shipwrecked hopes, points to Jesus ridding the Land of Rome's deranging effects (Matt 8:28–34). Jesus tells the demons, "Go," and they enter into a herd (a military term) of unclean swine and plunge into the sea (from which Rome originally came to Palestine). His focus here is not upon the miraculous, but upon how people can be delivered from traumatizing, contaminating imperial policies.

Today many need to be exorcised of the mental, social, psychological, and political demons that plague them, named: Anxiety, Depression, Paranoia, Psychosis, Addiction, Bigotry, Violence, and such. To cast these out, Jesus expects us to utilize the miracle of transformed hearts, of good governing, and the "miracles of modern medicine" which have advanced human physical, mental, socio/political, and economic well-being beyond what the first century could ever imagine. To expect Jesus to cure every aliment is to detract from the true purpose of his healings, which is to guarantee a decent, safe, holistic, and healthy world through human action.

My family has experienced the "miracle of modern medicine." At my daughter's birth, she developed hyaline membrane disease, an often fatal condition. The Kennedy's baby died of it during his presidency. Sandie and I prayed, our families prayed, our church prayed. I even made extravagant vows if God would pull my child through. The month our daughter was born, twenty-two children in Los Angeles County had the disease. We were told that our daughter was the only one who survived. To this day we call her our "miracle child."

Yet, I must exercise caution. What of the other twenty-one babies that died? Did God not hear the prayers offered for them? Did God treat me special because I was studying for the ministry? Or could it be that our sick daughter was under the care of a dedicated pediatrician, a personal friend, who spent much time watching over her and even resuscitated her once? I saw in this dedicated doctor the face of Jesus and the unusual caring miracle through whom Jesus gave my daughter life. Jesus shows up to fix things, but often through the hands of a caring doctor who facilitates divine healing.

Fifth, how much agony one endures may be linked to the availability and affordability of preventive or curative health care. The victim in the

Good Samaritan story is further harmed when two unmoved state bureaucrats ignore his plight and pass him by. Fortunately, an enemy possessed with a high character is "moved with compassion" for him and comes to his aid (Luke 10:30–37). The point is that God does not directly intervene to fix the man's misfortune. Rather, God expects those near him to do the right thing. Two fail, one succeeds. The Samaritan enemy becomes the face of God and God's miracle. It is like the song our choir sang every Mother's Day: "I see the face of God in your face; I feel the hands of God in your hands."

The moral: God expects the community to "love your neighbor as yourself" and to fix brokenness by meeting both immediate and long-term needs like the Samaritan does. For some hit by misfortune, government safety nets may be the true miracles they desperately need. We Christians need to be healed of our deafness and blindness to this truth about good governing that Jesus taught, modeled, and inaugurated.

Sixth, the meaning of Jesus' healings is captured in the word *shalom*. Jesus sends out his followers to the villages to "let your peace come upon it" (Matt 10:13); and this peace includes healings. While shalom ends external conflict and inner turmoil, it also brings "wholeness" and enhances human flourishing at the physical, social, religious, and economic levels (peace in any one area of life spills over to others, as captured in the holistic health movement). Biblical shalom is primarily a Kingdom or political value, best translated "the common good"—including the good that universal health care brings.

Our failures of faith stem from a misunderstanding of what Jesus came to do. He hopes to set every person, every institution, every nation on the right road, but never promises to fix all the potholes and the flat tires (although he gives us the good sense to carry a spare). Christians of character actively encourage and engage people, nations, and basic institutions to fulfill their missions—to fix a damaged world. To stand back and passively assume Jesus will fix all brokenness is to disparage our faith, our character, our mission, and the power of Jesus' Spirit to work through humans and their institutions. The showboating under the guise of miracle healings we see on the church channels is an offense to Jesus and Christianity. A Fix-all Jesus is actually a broken Jesus.

14
An Intolerant Jesus

Human history has bequeathed deep scars from horrendous forms of intolerance due to misplaced fears, which are never slow to construct dungeons of hate. This hatred births a festering brood of bigotries that strikes at human differences. Multitudes have gazed approvingly when heretics were burned, women "witches" were dunked, prisoners were guillotined, blacks were bought and sold and lynched, and Jews were rounded up, shot, and gassed. The Holocaust, with its unimaginable bloodbath, stands as a universal reminder of the ultimate consequence of even the slightest intolerance of out-groups. Unfortunately, some of the world's most respected Christian scholars not only watched but participated in such slaughter. We must never forget that Jesus was a Jew and to demean Jews is to demean Jesus. Some Christians today, under the label of "Messianic Jews," attempt to convert Jews to Christianity, yet another way Judaism is insulted. Judaism is Christianity's parent and to dishonor one's parent is to violate the Fifth Commandment.

Muslims, too, bear the brunt of religious intolerance. Islamophobia reaches deep into the hearts of many Christians, and their fears are easily exploited. One Florida pastor encouraged his people to burn the Koran in public while others vehemently oppose the building of mosques. Many colleges held an "Islamofascism Awareness Week" on their campuses. This highly-spiced term only reinforces prejudice against Muslims. What if someone started a campus lecture tour entitled, "Christofascism Awareness Week," where fascist tendencies of or atrocities initiated by Christian extremists were touted? Most Christians would be insulted. The same bigotry undergirds the phrase "Muslim terrorist," as if terrorism is necessarily

PART 1—BELITTLING JESUS

connected to Islam. Every religion has a sordid backstory. Fundamentalism, the enemy of tolerance and the higher human virtues, rears up in every major religion (and political ideology), including Christianity; and that is what needs to be countered at every sighting.

Even though this country was supposedly founded upon Christian principles, social intolerance toward minority groups slithered into American life and left its poisonous and festering bite. Native Americans were not considered fully human and were systematically slaughtered. The same ideology held Blacks in slavery and kept women and the landless from voting. These groups had no access to the cherished values of justice and freedom and they still bear the brunt and effects of discrimination. Now, Latino's are treated as unwelcome and pejoratively called "illegal aliens." "Illegal" usually refers to *acts* and not *people* and when coupled with "aliens," implies they are non-human invaders from outer space—adding further insult to injury.

An ongoing challenge for white America is the personal and institutional racism that plagues African Americans. One historian claims that because Christians justified slavery as divine mandate, they allowed this horrendous practice to persist as long as it did.[1] Billy Graham, and later Martin Luther King, Jr., decried that the most segregated hour in America is eleven a.m. Sunday. These shameful outcomes mandate that Christians especially work to undo the lingering wrong of our forefathers. Racism has left the sinister legacy that our brothers and sisters of color lag behind their white counterparts in almost every positive statistic, while leading in nearly every negative one.

Police shootings highlight the ongoing struggle of our society with racial fears, stereotypes, and discrimination. The Charleston Church gunman was steeped in a white supremacist ideology of genocide—that Blacks do not deserve to live. Tribalism runs deep in the American psyche and has become so institutionalized that it reduces a minority group's life chances, especially when facing competitive college entrance requirements, a tight job market, overzealous law enforcement, and a biased court system with its unfair incarceration rates. Whiteness in American society carries inordinate privilege and power, while blackness conveys stigma and exclusion. These are holes of which it is difficult to crawl out, and thus, the best whites

---

1. Reimers, *White Protestantism*, 183. "Indeed, the evidence suggests that white southern Protestantism helped prepare the white South for the full capitulation to racism."

can claim is that we are "recovering racists," while being challenged with the truth that "Black lives matter."

Women and children have borne the weight of discrimination from time's beginning. Women have been treated as second class citizens, with religion often playing a role in their oppression. Roman Catholicism and some denominations deny women ordination under the rubric that Jesus was a male or that woman must remain silent in the church. Christian Fundamentalists insist that a wife be subordinate to her husband who is the household's head and its bread winner. Her role is to be a homemaker. A Macho-Jesus only reinforces male status and privilege, opening up women to discrimination, mistreatment, beatings, and sexual assault. Ironically, one role thrust upon the homebound women is that of the "bearer of culture" or the "guardian of tradition." Early on young women are taught not only to accept and remain in their assigned status and roles, but also to defend them in the court of public opinion. Thus, Christian women can be the strongest opponents of women's rights.

These inequalities are grounded in outworn cultural creeds and faulty interpretations of a few biblical passages. Let's briefly examine a Pauline passage that refers to Jesus four times, but is often used to justify the subordination of women—Ephesians 5:22–33. This text, which speaks to the relationship between husband and wife, should actually begin with verse 21: "Be subject to one another out of reverence for Christ." Subjection is always mutual; never limited to only one party in any relationship. It is simply another way of stating what Jesus and Paul teach about subjecting our interests to those of others; i.e., practicing self-giving love out of "reverence for Christ," who did the same for us. "Subjection," then, is simply one other way of expressing *agape*, the term Christians chose to highlight the selfless/submissive element in love.

The second mention of Jesus refers to his being the "head of the church" as the model of husbands being the "head" *of* the wife (not *over* the wife). The meaning here is not our Western idea of "authority over" like the head of a company. Rather "head" means "source" like the head of a stream. The human head is the source for *nourishment* (food) and Paul specifically uses this sense of headship in vs. 29 where he again mentions Jesus and affirms that Christ, as head, "nourishes and tenderly cares" for the church. Had Paul meant the head imagery to justify male authority over the wife, he would contradict what he says in another letter, "For the wife does not have authority over her own body, but the husband does; *equally*, the husband

PART 1—BELITTLING JESUS

does not have authority over his own body, but the wife does" (1 Cor 7:4, italics mine). Note that Paul uses the word "equally" when discussing authority in marriage. Clearly for Paul, loving authority and its respectful submission *are always mutual.*

In a marriage, each partner carries special gifts with special expertise. For instance, my wife is a nurse and I defer to her authority when it comes to medical issues. I know so little about medicine that I mispronounce many medical terms, eliciting her occasional chuckle. Because of her encouragement to check out certain ailments, I am a two-time cancer survivor. On my part, having built five houses from scratch, I am somewhat skilled in construction. She defers to my authority when it involves fixing things around the house. In neither case, however, does our specialized authority become authoritarian. We encourage the other's input in all areas.

As a further nod to equality, Paul exhorts, "husbands should love (*agape*) their wives as their own bodies." This concrete application of Jesus' Golden Rule, confirms that husbands should, equally, act in love's self-sacrificing subjection to their wives. Even more, Paul refers to Jesus a fourth time, admonishing, "husbands love your wives, just as Christ loved the church and gave himself up for her." Jesus' sacrifice of his own interests for the church is the standard for the husband to *submit* his own male power and self-interests to those of his wife and the wife to her husband. So Paul's discussion ends where it began, "Be subject to (i.e., love and respect) one another (equally) out of reverence for Christ." When either husband or wife refuses to follow Jesus' nurturing and mutually submissive example, they belittle him, exhibit low character, and wither their marriage.

In a world of extreme gender inequality, Jesus models the equality of women by speaking to them in public, by standing up for them, by healing them, and by memorializing them, even if disreputable (John 4:7–30; 8:3–11; Mark 14:3–9; 5:25–34; Matt 21:31). Breaking strict custom, he honors a Gentile woman with: "Woman, great is your faith!" (Matt 15:21–28). By perpetuating the unequal treatment of women in any venue—home, society, workplace, church—Christians mistreat Jesus and nullify his message of tolerance.

A most important and undergirding moral notion in the Judeo-Christian faith is hospitality to strangers—those "strange" to us because they are unknown or different, not a part of the dominant community due to skin color, residence, religion, nationality, etc. The Leviticus 19 passage that contains the love your neighbor statute specifically commands the Israelite community to love the foreigner as they love themselves, reminding the citizens that they were once strangers in Egypt (Lev 19:34). Opening one's home and homeland to those different is the bedrock of Israel's constitution and brought the judgment of God when ignored (Gen 19:1–26; Judg 19:1—20:48; Isa 58:7). The mandate is relevant today: Christians should never treat undocumented workers or refuges as unwelcome, as walled out.

Back then the "cultural warriors," who pompously parade their pride and prejudice under the pretext of piety, criticize Jesus for welcoming and eating with (affirming) marginalized people (Luke 15:1–2). They are quick to distinguish themselves from those who are or act differently. They target Gentiles, Samaritans, women and children, the landless poor and hungry, the diseased, and those not up to snuff regarding expected customs and mores—the "sinners." By eating with unclean sinners, Jesus flaunts the honor/shame codes, while bestowing dignity upon them. Nevertheless, in the eyes of his characterless adversaries, he becomes unclean and also a "sinner." Jesus justifies his action with a parable about a welcoming father who becomes unclean when he, out of compassion, "puts his arms around and kisses" his pig-contaminated son. Here, Jesus exemplifies true moral purity by embracing the sullied unembraceable.

Welcoming strangers is one of the key planks of Jesus' mission when he sends his followers into the villages to initiate the coming Good Governing. He instructs them, "If anyone will not welcome you . . . shake off the dust from your feet as you leave the town." It will be "more tolerable for Sodom and Gomorrah on the day of judgment than for that town" (Matt 10:14–15). Not accepting the stranger/foreigner/immigrant/marginalized as full partners and citizens within the community could not be more severely rebuked by Jesus.

Jesus knows how people are traumatized and then stigmatized by adversities such as foreclosure, job loss, minor arrest, divorce, being born out of wedlock, childhood abuse, and the million other ways misery knocks. Added injury is heaped when members of minority groups—mostly dealt losing hands—are further degraded by being called derogatory names and blamed as authors of their own victimization. For disrupting the system's exclusionary norms and for welcoming all into his Beloved Community, Jesus is arrested, tried, convicted, sentenced, and crucified.

Jesus strongly opposes in-group superiority when he declares, "For all who exalt themselves will be humbled and all who humble themselves will be exalted" (Luke 14:11). Simply, but ironically put, Jesus is intolerant of intolerance, knowing that the evening shadows of prejudice inch into total darkness. He rejects his honor culture and stands by those despised, welcoming them and telling positive stories about them, which bring them standing and dignity. So forceful is Jesus in condemning packaged hate and its intolerance that any smidgen of prejudice and discrimination based upon race, religion, age, social strata, gender, nationality, housing status, sexual orientation, etc. is to slur Jesus himself—to mar his character and ours as well. Then, Christ is cast into a small-minded mold.

15
An End-times Jesus

A glaring misread of Jesus obsesses over his role in a future, preordained, and cataclysmic end of Planet Earth. World-ending apocalypticism is found in nearly every religion, especially those that believe in a future heaven and hell. It prevails in American Christianity, driven by a literally followed timeline popularized by the Scofield Bible, the rise of Dallas Theological Seminary, the Bible school movement, Hal Lindsey's, *The Great Late Planet Earth* book, and the wildly popular, *Left Behind* fiction series. Most Televangelists readily address future events; some fixate upon them. Best known as "Dispensationalism," the movement, driven by biblical literalism, neatly divides history into seven separate periods or dispensations, each in which God acts differently.

A focus upon the end times is driven by speculation surrounding the Second Coming of Christ: what are the signs of his imminent coming; how will he come; how will he rule and for how long; and what happens to the good and bad people? Throwing caution to the wind, some have set specific dates for Christ's return, the most notorious being Harold Campy of Family Radio. His numerous predictions of the Lord's return have, of course, always turned out wrong. Yet, many more are quick to read the signs of the times. We do a great disservice to Jesus, the Bible, and Christianity when we attempt to pawn specific timelines, claim hidden codes, or predict contemporary events from the Bible. Let's heed Jesus: "False prophets will appear and produce signs and omens, to lead astray, if possible, the elect" (Mark 13:22).

The marvelous truth regarding Jesus' return is not the speculative signs or dates, but his coming into the lives of Christians and our institutions, through whom and for whom all things have been created and all things hold together (Col 1:15–17). Christians look to continue his Kingdom on Earth that dawned 2000 years ago and is still coming to full light. Those who enter it are needy people—those wracked with physical and mental pain; those who lack food, water, clothing, and shelter; and those treated inhospitably and considered inferior or outcasts. Jesus assures that his "return" comes "with great power and glory" to an ailing world and the barren hearts that long for his presence. He comes when we partner with him in his Kingdom efforts to guarantee a sustainable human community and Earth far into the future.

Correctly, Dispensationalists believe that apocalyptic notions touch today's politics. However, their contemporary references are fanciful and often reinforce more Conservative social and political ideals. Ironically, apocalyptic thinking emerged as a literary device to oppose the Conservative imperial rule with its devastating effects upon the occupied masses. It allowed people in seemingly hopeless situations to express their anger as well as their dreams. Employing extravagant imagery, this type of literature thunders a radical reversal of prevailing political values. The book of Daniel speaks to eliminating despotic empires in its day, while Revelation addresses oppressive Roman rule and records the most explosive denunciations of imperialism in Western literature. Describing Rome as the kingdom of Satan and likening it to scary beasts and whores bespeaks treason.

Jesus, in fact, uses apocalyptic language to counter both the savagery of Rome and violence of the common Messianic resistance movements: "And if anyone says to you at that time, 'Look! Here is the Messiah!' or 'Look! There he is!'—do not believe it." For Jesus, one must "beware" of persecutions; and "the one who endures to the end will be saved." Proper bloodless resistance means "you will stand before governors and kings because of me and as a testimony to them." For Jesus, then, change comes nonviolently, i.e., not by killing kings, but by "testimony to them." Words are powerful, dethroning, and enduring since "heaven and Earth may pass away, but my words will not pass away" (Mark 13:9–31).

In this light, contemporary applications of Jesus' prophetic and apocalyptic nonviolent resistance are most appropriately directed against any corporate power that attempts to impose its will upon the weak and then reinforce it with state violence. Ironically, some interpreters of Revelation use its imagery to justify extreme nationalism and its by-product, militarism—the very values that Jesus attempts to undercut. America's ethnocentrism and exceptionalism often orchestrate apocalyptic judgments against our enemies, while blinding us to our own misuses of power.

Similarly, because of their misreading of end times, some tend to uncritically support Israel and have little sympathy for valid Palestinian land claims. However, we must exercise caution regarding the emergence of Israel as a sure sign that Jesus' second coming is near. Yet, any critique of Israel must show understanding and sensitivity given the Holocaust, history's greatest scourge. The purpose of apocalyptic was to question the overreach of nations, no matter which ones. Futile speculations and misguided theologies only perpetuate historical injustices.

The Dispensationalist's most foreboding figure is the Antichrist—Christ's fraudulent antitype. Of course, Christian pundits in the know are quick to expose this deceiver. The political leaders these end-timers despise (usually liberals) are labelled the Antichrist, especially those who tolerate homosexuality and abortion (practices that also signal the end-days). Pick your political enemy and you have your Antichrist. As anticipated, some extremists considered Obama the Antichrist.

In response, the Antichrist, as the name conveys, is anything or anyone who stands against what Jesus stood for. Jesus opposed wealth for the few when the many were in poverty; he opposed excluding people because they did not meet social expectations; he opposed the hierarchies of status; and he denounced militarism and nationalism. What a breathtaking irony, that these very anti-Jesus values often reside in those who warn of the Antichrist. In truth, we all possess some Antichrists lurking deeply in our souls, and why we are always in need of humble repentance.

Apocalypticism finds its home in contemporary theology, but not in the way end-time Christians might think. Because it expresses the grievances of oppressed peoples and provides a measure of hope, it warns us, given our American Exceptionalism, of the unthinkable devastation wrought by weapons of mass destruction. Also its startling imagery, derived mostly from natural upheavals, is compelling when applied to our ecological crises. Unfortunately, most end-timers have little interest in the future of our Earth. For instance, James Watt, a former Secretary of the Interior, believed that Jesus' imminent return renders environmental concerns moot. Nevertheless, if nations continue saber rattling or ravaging the environment, global catastrophe is inevitable. This nonchalant end-time thinking poses an apocalyptic mega-danger of a barren or blown apart Planet.

Thank God, Jesus does not herald a cataclysmic end to the world, but rather an end to the pervasive imperial rule that makes life unbearable for so many. To link Jesus to end-time schemes or to argue about a pre- or post-Tribulation misses the point of Jesus' concern for the future and belittles his purpose. What exalts Jesus is to discover ways to preserve the world from our folly. Thus, eschatology should become a branch of theology that addresses the ways to make life on Earth more sustainable and nonviolent for future generations. Regarding specific predictions, Jesus unequivocally declares, "About that day or hour no one knows, neither the angels in heaven, nor the Son . . ." (Mark 13:32). All our speculations about end-times assume we can know more than Jesus on this matter, betraying hyper-arrogance—yet another way we humiliate him and leave character in ruins.

16
A Flag-waving-warrior Jesus

Most end-time Christians strongly believe that God has chosen America to be special among nations—a city on the hill, a light to all peoples, referred to as "American Exceptionalism." Since the American way of life is considered "superior," some feel justified in imposing our cultural values upon others, even by military might. These Christians are super-patriot flag-wavers and link their nationalistic and "might makes right" values to their faith. Often American flags adorn their church sanctuaries (along with a red, white, and blue Christian flag), symbolizing an unbreakable connection between loving God and loving country. Indeed, American flags began appearing in churches during World War I and II to provide religious sanction to those wars. The flags remained after the wars ended, further encouraging the link of patriotism/militarism to Christianity. This super-patriotism translates into never ceding an ounce of sovereignty to international bodies. Yet, is this not another form of prideful "exaltation" that counters the mind of Christ and tarnishes Christian and the national character?

While Christians should love their country and be loyal to it, true patriots do not blindly endorse "my country, right or wrong." Those who love their country stand ready to challenge its missteps, as a loving parent does for its child. Jesus too, loves Israel with such passion that he willingly becomes its suffering servant and dies for it. Yet, like the prophets of old, he believes that Israel's exile (now under Rome) resulted from its leaders submitting to imperial values. In railing against Rome's surrogate leaders for their injustices, he hopes to redeem Israel so it can fulfill its mission of being a saving light to the nations. For Jesus, this means leaders become servants—serving the needs of its citizens and of other nations (Mark 10:42). Yet, it is difficult for a nation to be a light in the darkness, when it, too, gropes around in shades of grey.

Heart wrenching as it may be, unspeakable violence has often been sanctified as "holy war." Recently, a few have attempted to portray Jesus as attuned to violence, believing that the Kingdom will come with force when he says, "I have not come to bring peace, but a sword."[1] However, here Jesus uses "sword" metaphorically in the context of family conflict, confirmed when Luke substitutes "division" for "sword" (Matt 10:34 with Luke 12:5). More in line with Jesus' view is his statement, "For all who take the sword will perish by the sword" (Matt 26:52). In a weapons-obsessed, warmongering culture, Jesus counters with, "Blessed are the peacemakers" (Matt 5:9).

Unfortunately, his later professed followers took a page from Caesar's book of blood and tortured and killed fellow Christians over minor infractions or deviations in doctrine, started wars against perceived pagans, and generally accepted violence as a necessary means to preserve a way of life. Earth drinks deep from the blood spilled under religious banners. It is ironic and tragic that atrocities could ever occur under a Christian banner.

Many Christians have eschewed violence and adopted some form of pacifism modeled upon Jesus' life. It is difficult; however, to be an *absolute* pacifist, given the horrors of powerful nations like Nazi Germany. Early Christians recognized the inevitability of violence and attempted to place strict moral conditions upon its use. Their selective pacifism became known as Just War Theory, specifically designed to *limit* violence. Engaging in war could only be justified to defend against aggression, and then only after all reasonable attempts to resolve the conflict have been exhausted. Furthermore, Just War criteria attempt to limit how a war is conducted so that noncombatants are protected, prisoners of war are treated fairly, appropriate means are used to gain objectives, etc. The upshot: if all parties could agree to these criteria, war would forever be abolished.

Regrettably, most Christians have never been taught the Just War tradition. During my twenty years of teaching ethics in a seminary, I would initially ask students to name the Just War criteria. Only a few students could name one or two of its principles. Most had never even heard of Christian Just War theory or could not recall it ever being referenced in their church. Thus, it is understandable why our government does not expect an outcry from American Christians when it declares war. Regardless,

---

1. Aslan, *Zealot*, 120.

when nations justify going to war, collective self-interest usually prevails. Bogus justifications for violence often trump the Just War criteria or the principles are so misinterpreted as to be rendered moot.

Some Christians even embrace a "Crusader ethic" that undermines Just War ideals. This ethic provides quick and convenient justification for attacking other countries, based upon revenge, persevering economic interests, or anticipating a country's future threat. Predictably, these more nationalistic and militaristic-oriented Christians also reject the role of international bodies like the United Nations in resolving conflicts. A few even suggest the UN represents the future evil world government predicted by their misshapen end-times schemes. This anti-internationalism is doubly frightening in an age in which nations stockpile weapons of mass destruction. Jesus taught us to settle disputes in nonviolent cooperative ways. He is one of the few founders of a religion who never engaged in violence or warfare. Trusting in nationalism and military might is not a biblical ideal, and thus, should never be a Christian one (Jer 9:23). Attitudes of national supremacy differ little in dynamics from white supremacy.

A spin-off of the Warrior Jesus and closer to home is the Tough-love Jesus who takes up the switch as a means to discipline children. James Dobson and his Focus on the Family organization believes that, on occasion, a little violence can be an effective way to raise children.[2] However, scientific research has shown that generally spanking is not effective, and, in fact, counterproductive. Jesus always shows the greatest respect for children and insists no one should "harm these little ones"; they are models for entering the Kingdom (Matt 18:3–6). What children actually learn when hit by a parent is that violence is an acceptable strategy for imposing one's will.[3] Beginning in the home, this violence continues onto the playground and then upon one's own children, one's spouse, or one's national enemies. To spank a child, under the rubric of discipline, is to belittle the children Jesus exalted, and thus, to belittle Jesus.

Jesus admonishes us to "love your enemies," a phrase not found anywhere else in ancient literature. This extraordinary love means: "Do good to those who hate you." He outright rejects the scriptural retaliation law, telling people, "Do not resist an evil doer. But if anyone strikes you on the right cheek, turn the other also" (Matt 5:38–48). When Christians blindly promote America's culture of guns and violence, they undercut the higher

---

2. Dobson, *The New Dare*, 61–65.
3. Gershoff, "Spanking," 133–37.

values that Jesus taught and for which he died. He longs for a world, not based upon revenge and retaliation, but one grounded in unconditional forgiveness and kindness—even to an enemy. We are then "perfect" like God whose sun rises on the evil and on the good, and sends rain on the righteous and unrighteous" (Luke 6:27-36). A sword-wielding faith cuts Jesus down to a very small size and reveals a serious character flaw.

17
A Subdue-our-Earth Jesus

Christians have always appreciated God's created Earth, since God has declared it "good." The Psalmist celebrates Earth as manifesting the glory of God and displaying God's marvelous handiwork (Ps 19:1–6). The more science establishes the incredible intricacies of the Universe, whether seen through a microscope or a telescope, the more we are awestruck. The Hebrew faith revolutionized religion by seeing God as transcending the Universe, its minerals and forces. According to some, this achievement brought an ecological downside. Because divinity was separated from stones and water and trees and storms and animals, the worship of earthen objects (idolatry) was forbidden. Losing their inherent sacredness, the elements could be exploited without regard to the ecological consequences. In addition, some Christians allegedly interpret the passage in Genesis about "subduing" Earth as justifying its plunder.[1]

Exploiting Earth without restraint had little practical effect for millennia when its carrying capacity faced little threat, although this permitted imperial bad habits to persist. Now with burgeoning population and our relentless and insatiable American madness to produce and consume without end, our writhing Earth faces a dire, pollution-filled future. Some irreversible tipping points have already arrived.

The view that God has mandated Earth to be subdued, treated as a commodity, and used as its owners, producers, and consumers see fit finds traction in states that depend heavily upon the coal and oil industries. Indeed, Christians often follow the cultural and economic creeds of

---

1. White, "The Historical Roots," 1205.

their regions, irrespective of whether they can reconcile such notions with overwhelming counter-evidence, or even a biblical ethic. The crucial fight now waged is over human-induced climate change. Some Christians are climate-change deniers, reinforced by their already strong anti-science attitudes and anti-government stance. They see little connection between walking in the footsteps of Jesus and making those footsteps smaller and less carbon intensive. End-time Christianity contributes to inaction by seeing the world's destruction as divinely ordained, and thus, inevitable. Little do they accept the truth that human greed could render an apocalyptic end a frightening possibility.

Jesus was handed a Hebrew Land legacy out of which sprouted the peoples' very existence and nursed their faith and hope. Grounded in the Creation story, Israel's earliest creed promised a "land flowing with milk and honey"; i.e., enough to sustain the whole community (Deut 26:5–9). But Israel's corrupt leaders misused the Land's sustainability ethic. Jesus sprinkles his parables with Nature imagery that speaks to violating subsistence values. A prodigal son eschews his life-sustaining Land and "squandered his property in dissolute living." A rich man gorges himself while "at his gate lay a poor man named Lazarus, covered with sores, who longed to satisfy his hunger with what fell from the rich man's table." The fig tree languishes because no one will "dig around it and put manure upon it." A hoarding rich man contemplates, "I will build larger barns to store my grain and my goods." Wicked tenants appropriate an owner's vineyard and conspire to "kill the heir so that the inheritance may be ours" (Luke 15:13; 16:20–21; 20:14; 13:8; 12:18).

Jesus' saying that God makes the "sun rise upon the evil and the good and sends rain upon the righteous and the unrighteous" acknowledges God's power over and loving distribution of Nature's vital resources (Matt 5:45). Jesus shows the same loving authority within Nature when he says to the sea, "Peace! Be still!" and when he walks on water. Facing myriads of hungry people, he instructs his disciples, "You give them something to eat" and distributes to them the Land's produce, linking the dawning Kingdom to the ancient promise of a sustaining fruitful Land (Mark 4:35–41; Matt 14:13–33 with Deut 26:9).

We know that someday in God's grand plan and own time the Sun will implode and Earth will be destroyed in a flash. Yet, God never intended for humans to destroy all it habitats and inhabitants by willful neglect, ignorance, and unrelenting greed. Jesus inherits the prophetic view that exile and ecological disaster result when the leadership profanes the "holy" Land by selfishly taking all its bounty, leaving the masses languishing (Isa 5:1–30). To ignore Creation-care while claiming to serve Jesus is to profane Earth, desecrate its Creator and Lord, and sully Christian character.

18
A Wing-nut Jesus

In all probability, this chapter and its counterpart (chapter 33) may be the most controversial sections of this book. They speak to politics, which is an especially contentious and emotional subject, rivaling Christianity's shameful religious disputes. As a Baptist pastor, I could preach to my people and call them "damned sinners," and might hear a chorus of "amens." But if I called them "damned Democrats" or "damned Republicans," all hell would break loose.

America today lies battered by divisiveness and cynicism, enmeshed in a nasty ongoing war of words as we endure hour upon hour of vitriolic talk radio and popular "news" channels. Battle lines have been drawn between competing political ideas and value systems, pushing people to the far left or right edges of the political spectrum, as illustrated in the 2016 election. Christians, too, are caught in this war zone, leaving them deeply divided on the critical issues of the day. Tragically, a few Christians are so extreme that they resort to violence like murdering abortion doctors or Norway's July 22nd mass murderer.

Many Evangelical Christians have cast their lot on the political right, named the "Religious Right." They are so forceful in American political life that candidates go to great lengths to solicit their support. Their concerns focus primarily upon "family values," including hot-button issues like preserving the more traditional roles of women, opposing abortion and euthanasia, rejecting homosexuality, and promoting "religious freedom." Christian "values voters" find a natural home in a broader conservative agenda which battles creeping secularism, unlimited tolerance, government overreach, and internationalism—all linked to liberalism.

A Wing-nut Jesus

Jesus entered a world also divided by extreme political values. Back then, politics was interwoven with religion, making it impossible to separate the two. In another book, I attempt to show that Jesus embarks upon a political mission to "redeem Israel" and; therefore, his sayings and parables speak primarily to national issues (Luke 24:21).[1] His most famous phrase, "Kingdom of God," has highly political overtones and includes the renewal of the ancient Mosaic Constitution—Israel's nation-building document. The attempts throughout history to de-politicize Jesus' Kingdom notion distorts his message. In opposition, he articulates those values that constitute good governing, while opposing Rome's onerous imperial mores.

Most of the political/religious parties and movements that Jesus criticizes (Pharisees, Sadducees, Essenes, Herodians, and proto-Zealots) embraced many of the malignant imperial values: hierarchy and status, luxury, strict law and order, national superiority, and militarism. These parties unearthed such values somewhere in their Scripture. Jesus, however, reads the Bible differently and faces continuing opposition from the Conservative cultural warriors in their drive for status, their accumulating of wealth in the midst of destitution, their showy rituals, their worship of narrow purity and Sabbath creeds that exclude "undesirables," and their willingness to use violence in solving problems. In defiance, he defends the poor and honors "unclean" outcasts. As noted above, Jesus also critiques the rural resistance that uses the same imperial values to raise its sword against Rome. Given the moral/political bankruptcy as well as the futility of violence when facing Rome's Legions, his famous saying about rejecting the sword is not only good practical morality, but also a well-crafted political truth (Matt 26:52).

The enculturated values that Jesus opposed are all tied to individual and collective egoism. They wend their way through history and find their counterparts under the wave of contemporary banners, one of which is a strident Conservatism. American Conservatives support hierarchies and tolerate great social and economic gaps. They believe private property is nearly sacrosanct and should be bought, sold, and used as owners see fit with minimal government regulation. They also tend to embrace the American individualistic mindset as we have described and believe that America is superior to all other nations, is especially blessed by God, and must be buttressed by a military second to none. Most Christians who support a Conservative values agenda see themselves as the last defense

---

1. See Miller, *Jesus Goes to Washington*, 41–50, for a discussion of the politics of Jesus.

PART 1—BELITTLING JESUS

against a deteriorating American culture—society's "tradition warriors," so to speak.² Pharaoh and Caesar are names of old, but their imperial character and its crimes never age; they simply operate under different aliases.

Jesus rejects the extreme right and violent left wings of his world. He dramatically rephrases the definitive edict on national holiness, "You shall be holy," by substituting "compassion" for "holy" (Lev 19:2 with Luke 6:36). True holiness is suffering with those enduring overly harsh imperial principles and the resulting violence. As mentioned above, Jesus does advocate one extreme view for his day—"love your enemies." He unpacks its meaning with: "do not resist an evil doer"; "if anyone strikes you on the right cheek, turn the other also"; "if anyone wants to sue you and take your coat, give your cloak as well"; "if anyone forces you to go one mile, go also the second mile"; and "give to everyone who begs from you, and do not refuse anyone who wants to borrow from you" (Matt 5:38–48). This enemy-love makes one "perfect," but is so exceptional that the phrase cannot be found anywhere else in ancient literature, although the idea undergirds the Hebrew Scripture (Exod 23:4; Lev 19:33).³

Jesus' extravagant love counters all far-out politics grounded in the blights of revenge, hierarchy, tight-handedness, and violence with their unbroken chain of human and Earth woe. He opposes that which breathes fire on the immigrant, or thrusts its pitchfork into the heart of the gay man, or whose tail swats at the forlorn houseless person on the way by. To identify Jesus with extreme right wing or left wing views is to mar his basic mission, and thus, to render him and us extremely small-minded.

In summary, we have examined many ways Jesus is belittled by the popular theology of many professing Christians. Again, we affirm that most of the above caricatures include a sprout of truth. Yet, when they overwhelm other dimensions, they choke out the richness of Jesus for one's own spirituality as well as trivialize him in the eyes of potential believers. In truth, all the distortions listed above are forms of idolatry—worshipping a false god. In humility, all Christians must confess that we miniaturize Jesus every day in some way or another. None of us can escape our humanity and its infused self-absorption, reinforced by the all-pervasive American Character. Temptations always lurk and we are remarkably clever at self-justification, even if it results in humiliating our Lord and Savior. And a diminished Jesus guarantees the collapse of Christian character. From this

2. O'Reilly, *Cultural Warrior*, 77.
3. Meier, *A Marginal Jew*, 532–51.

infectious human tragedy, we need to repent, accept God's generous (gracious) healing forgiveness through the exalted Jesus, and, with the Spirit's power incorporate the very character of Jesus and live the Christ-minded life worthy of that forgiveness.

In the next section, we shall present the more exalted Jesus, one truer to his words within Scripture. We will herald the heaven-high values he showed by his character and actions. Hopefully, this opens the way for a growing and empowering moral character within us that reaches broader and higher, that embodies the compassionate mind of Christ, and that presents a more credible Christianity for all seekers.

PART 2
EXALTING JESUS

From Paul we learn that Jesus brought heaven's compassionate humility to Earth by his obedience to God's will through sacrificial service to and redemption of humanity. His high moral character clashed with the imperial mindset and led to his crucifixion. However, God stamps Jesus' humble obedience to serve with divine approval by highly exalting him. Because the lower values still prevail and impact our moral sense, our goal today is to scale the moral heights by forming Jesus' compassionate character within us, within the church, and within all our institutions. To know what Jesus would do means to first embody who Jesus is; i.e., reflect his essential character. This compels us to backpack with him on the dusty roads of Palestine to watch how he lived and hear what he taught and then act as he acts. The journey, though, is rough and includes the strain and pain of shedding our *childish* conceptions of faith (yet not our *childlike* expressions) for a more mature understanding along with Christ's instilled and towering moral character. Then, *because of the way we live*, the good news is launched and Christ is exalted in the sight of all (Phil 1:20).[4]

Yet, how do we exalt Jesus? In bowing before him, we affirm his mission and are driven to the broad ethical transformations needed in our lives and our society. Our repenting from the world's ways is more than discarding some personal bad habits. Of course, addictions can be quite serious, necessitating radical change. Jesus can be a powerful antidote. But biblical conversion is more than personal touchups. One could achieve sobriety, yet still hold toxic moral views—still be racist or self-aggrandizing. True conversion is incorporating the *full* mind/character of Christ that subdues our

---

4. Fowler, *Stages of Faith*, 199–211.

selfish nature and casts aside the deeply ingrained Americanized overlords with their popularly accepted suit-my-fancy agendas—a lifelong endeavor. Furthermore, our changed character must take flight into the realms of economic, ecological, and social justice. Jeremiah says it forthrightly: to "know" God is to support the cause of the poor (Jer 22:18). The prophet Micah defines the "good" that the Lord "requires" of us as "doing justice"— a justice supplemented by loving kindness and humility (Mic 6:8). Part 2 explores these themes.

Ironically, the Lordship of Christ is based upon his "obedient" servanthood, overcoming Adam's (humanity's) innate disobedience (Phil 2:8). Thus, while Luther pushed "faith alone," Paul talks about the "obedience of faith" (Rom 1:5). He states empathically, "*The only thing that counts* is faith made effective by love" (Gal 5:6, italics mine). James insists upon obedience when he says, "faith without works is dead" (the reason Luther shunned James). James further defines "true and undefiled religion" as visiting widows and following the "royal" law of loving one's neighbor as oneself. He specifically describes this love as being "unstained by the world"—a world of "favoritism" or selfish hierarchical arrangements that degrade those with less status. For him, neighbor-loving acts of obedience take precedence over all other religious activities (Jas 1:27—2:1–9). John adds that obediently loving one's brother and sister is a *marker* of true salvation, not just a *result* of it (1 John 3:11–23). These epistles faithfully mirror Jesus' humble and obedient service on our behalf and why obedience in fulfilling the loving opportunities life presents to us is a key marker of Christian character.

Because the Kenosis hymn specifically mentions that Jesus' earthly obedience leads to a "cross" (Rome's way of punishing sedition), his humble compassion and high exaltation invades the *political sphere*. Jesus opposes and subverts the sharp thorns of imperial polices, thorns that eventually find their nesting on his head. Yet, his execution was imperialism's death knell. Co-opting imperial language, the hymn celebrates his exaltation by opposing every power that grasps for divine status and holds on with all its might. By placing Jesus' name above every other name, *the hymn explicitly dishonors Caesar's name and any arrogant corporate power.*

Who ever heard of monarchs emptying themselves of their most high status, their power and wealth, their honor, their "divine" perks, and then sacrificially serving the interests of the masses—to the point of death? The Lord Jesus' obedient servant-rule over the whole world results in unmasking and replacing "Lord" Caesar's oppressive reign within the Mediterranean world. All "glory" goes to God the Father, and none to Caesar who mistakenly calls himself "Father of the Family." Every knee will gladly bow to Jesus' alternative compassionate and serving rule, and that includes Caesar's reluctant knee. No wonder this hymn was quite subversive to Roman values—the godparent to similar Conservative values now.

How does this political thrust relate to Paul's ethical concern of living a life worthy of Christ's gospel? Note that the word Paul uses for "live your life" is "*politeuesthe*," a pointedly political term (Phil 1:27). Thus, Paul's main concern is that we live our "political lives" in a manner worthy of the good news of the political Messiah (the meaning of "Christ"). To possess the compassionate "mind of Messiah" means we confront a Caesar-like mindset, governed by imperial self-exaltation with its clamor for status, power, wealth, and honor—the false "lords" that reign in and over us all. For Paul, Jesus' Caesar-defying incarnation, servant obedience to God, and death on the cross point to radical ethical transformation, not only within individuals, but also *within every social, economic, and political structure*. Then, and only then, is Jesus *fully* exalted and *fully* confessed as Lord.

Thus, when Jesus' compassion becomes ours, we obediently set aside our distorted imperial values and humbly and obediently embody a *public* mind that speaks the needed words to government and acts to relieve misery in all possible ways, even if unseasoned, even if crowned by thorns. In doing so, we proclaim Christ's Lordship over everything, including our political beliefs. Furthermore, when Christians talk of "biblical justice," they are thrust into the middle of political realities since only government can guarantee justice. Nevertheless, the crucial question is, "What *kind* of politics did Jesus have in mind that we are to emulate?" Answering that for today shall percolate throughout the following chapters.

Part 2 paints a more realistic and exalted portrait of Jesus underbrushed by insights from contemporary biblical studies, knowledge of the ancient Mediterranean world, and the social, economic, religious, and political context of his day. This more reliable picture of his life shows us the good news that humility and compassion are God's answers to the human predicament and the foundation for character building. This expanded portrait of Jesus also helps free us from our captivity to a Jesus created by the American culture, to one strong-armed by popular preachers, or to one that perpetuates our never-ending "selfish ambition" (Phil 2:3). Then, we can accord Jesus the dignity he fully deserves and live that dignity out in our lives, confirming that he is exalted above the lords of every self-centered pursuit and cultural mindset. Knees will bow to Jesus in praise and rise up to follow him in radical discipleship.

We shall also explore more deeply the words and phrases Paul uses in his Philippians letter to describe the mind/character of the one we desire to emulate. These include: "suffering," "joy," "the same love," "compassion and sympathy," "sharing in the Spirit," "humility," "the interests of others," "servant," "human form and likeness," "obedient unto death," "cross," "exalted," "name above all names," "Lord," and "glory,"—all building blocks for developing Christian character. We invite you to see what Jesus did for his world, so we can do the same for ours.

19
The Galilean-peasant Jesus

The Christian Church has not only confessed that Jesus is both God and human, it has insisted that he is *fully* divine and *fully* human. Unfortunately, the fully human part has often been short-changed in favor of his divine nature. As noted above, due to early christological controversies, his life, teachings, and mission were omitted in the early creeds. Of course, the creedalists wanted to assure his divinity by highlighting his miracle birth, saving death, and resurrection. As we suggest later, by downplaying his humanity, they actually undercut his divinity as well.

To comprehend Jesus as fully human, we must see his historical mission within the first-century matrix. The Kenosis hymn sings that Jesus was "born in human likeness" and was "found in human form" (Phil 2:7). He came immersed in his world, engaging in family dynamics, religious traditions, village interactions, regional social and economic issues, and the political forces at work in all of these. More specifically, appreciating his humanity compels us to consider his Galilean upbringing in a small village called Nazareth, his peasant culture, his commitment to Judaism, and his calling as a prophet dedicated to serve Israel's God-ordained destiny of being a light to the nations. By exploring his life and mission from these angles, we see the bigger picture of him and gain a clearer understanding of his character and how it shapes ours. In this chapter we shall explore his Galilean peasant roots and in the next his Jewish prophetic influences.

As a reminder, in Jesus' world religion, politics, economics, and ethics could never be separated. American Christians may find these connections alien since we insist upon the separation of church and state. Back then, the values held sacred by the Jews reached deeply into every realm of life,

PART 2—EXALTING JESUS

including the political arena. The religious leaders are also the political leaders and vice versa and each party believes it has the true answer for Israel's political restoration. The religious, political, and economic centerpiece of Palestine is the Jerusalem Temple, More accurately, it is a "Temple-state" where the Sanhedrin council (the religious leaders) meets and rules. It also serves as the major bank. The outlying synagogues also blur the distinction between political assembly and worship.

Both the individual and the national character were imbedded in traditional values. For example, the command to love your neighbor, found at the heart of Israel's Constitution, refers primarily to *civic* love (Lev 19:18). So when Jesus quotes it, he prefaces it with "Hear, O Israel..." (Mark 12:29). Jesus affirms that this greatest of all laws is *national* policy; it is primarily political, although Christians usually apply it in only personal ways. For Jesus, however, *civic* love takes front stage.

As a peasant, Jesus' menial (humble) status shapes how he looks at life, how he interprets his nation's Constitution and its religious traditions, and how they should be applied. First, he identifies with the poor masses and their unremitting drudgery. His spirit-filled calling is to "bring good news to the poor" and assures them that "yours is the kingdom of God" (Luke 4:18, 6:20). He seizes upon the so-called "little traditions" in Scripture that support the interests of little people, as opposed to the "official traditions" that justify the interests of the elite.

Second, he promotes the peasant moral economy and the "subsistence ethic" upon which it is based. Given the peasants' harsh conditions, subsistence values (1) assure the right to basic necessities when others possess an overabundance; (2) guarantee that villagers look out for one another and share even during times of scarcity; (3) assume a rough equality, even when great social and economic gaps exist; and (4) point to a future of social and economic inversion or reversal—the hope of a great turnaround.[1] Throughout history, these subsistence values have been at war with the imperial ethic that flatters our most malignant passions—hierarchy, luxury, cultural purity, nationalism, and militarism. Jesus speaks his mind based upon these ancient peasant values—values that feed today's sustainability ethic, our only hope for a viable human community and a healed planet.

The subsistence ethic leads him to admonish a rich ruler, "If you wish to be perfect, go, sell all your possessions, and give the money to the poor," and to commend a state bureaucrat (tax collector) who restores ill-begotten

1. Scott, *The Moral Economy*, 13–55.

gains to the peasants with: "Today, salvation has come to this house." The subsistence reversal is expressed in his sayings, "The last will be first and the first will be last" and "all who exalt themselves will be humbled and those who humble themselves will be exalted" (Matt 19:21; 20:16; Luke 14:11; 19:9–10).

Subsistence values permeate the Mosaic Charter, the Psalms, Proverbs, and the Prophets, reaching back to humanity's dawn and giving rise to the ancient question, "Am I my brother's keeper?" Israel's imperial rulers continually violate the peasant brother/sister keeper rule, leading ultimately to Israel's Exile. The prophet Samuel describes imperialism as an endless "take . . . take . . . take . . ." from the peasants (1 Sam 8:11–18). Early on, Solomon neglected the subsistence ethic and exploited the Northern tribes, resulting in a divided kingdom. Jesus being a "northerner," from Galilee, holds little regard for the policies of the "southern" Temple-state's surrogate leaders, who roll out Rome's imperial anti-subsistence scrolls upon the citizenry. The peasant moral economy justifies resistance in the face of gross unfairness, especially when human survival is at stake. However, Jesus rejects violence, choosing more "hidden" or subtle forms of nonviolent resistance through parables, enigmatic sayings, and symbolic actions.

Galilee was a breadbasket region, but Rome, like a hungry jackal, tore the heart out of peasant life with its draining taxes, confiscating of land, and undercutting of subsistence ideals. Roman imperial values plunges them into a downward spiral, wrapping them in a cloak of gloom and woe, mostly untold. Losing their ancestral farming land, they end up tenant farming, piecemeal day laboring, or survival's bleakest choices—begging or banditry. This onerous descent into a bottomless pit kindles Jesus' indignation. From the day of his birth into a peasant family, he champions subsistence principles to meet the basic needs of the hard-pressed. His catch phrase "the Kingdom of God" is shorthand for describing what God has in mind to defeat the blight of imperial values with its torrent of grief and restore governing values that serve the masses and bless the nations.

Ingrained imperial and cultural factors such as the Roman client/patron system, the Mediterranean honor/shame codes, eating arrangements, and ritual practices were the masonry that held the empire together while sustaining elite hierarchy with its wealth and privilege. Jesus counters these establishment norms on every hand with his sustainability values. In his parables, the wealthy invitees to the Messianic Banquet are left out in the cold, in favor of the houseless. A rich man ends up in "Hades" because of his callousness to a starving man. Rich nations are cast into "eternal fire" for shredding the safety net for the poor (Luke 14:24; 16:23; Matt 25:41). It would be hard to imagine more stinging denunciations of the prevailing social and economic realities bore by misery-ridden Galileans.

Jesus' peasant/Galilean context sheds a broader ray upon him and enhances our appreciation of his humanity, helping us to better understand his moral mission on Earth. Furthermore, it connects his earthly purposes to the urgencies of our callings today. His peasant-informed moral tools are especially compelling as we struggle with the same everyday "tyrannies" that he faced, such as the large gap between rich and poor, discrimination toward minority groups, pervasive violence, and Earth's woes. Possessing this humble Galilean peasant's character within us allows us to live, more fully, a life of sustainability worthy of the gospel, thereby exalting him. Yet, we further exalt him when we live him as a Jewish prophet.

20
The Jewish-Prophet Jesus

A key influence in Jesus' teachings and humble life is his Jewish heritage. His parents ingrained all the Jewish traditions and aspirations in his heart which strengthened his commitment to subsistence values and gave rise to his prophetic calling. He seizes upon a Hebrew view of God who "sees," "hears," and "knows" the afflictions of oppressed peoples—a God so different, so radical, so empathetic that God requires a new name— "Yahweh" (Exod 6:2–8). Like in Egypt, this compassionate God will liberate Israel from its internal Roman exile when its leaders shed imperial values and care for the peasant masses. Jesus addresses this empathetic God as "Our Father," echoing the Psalmist who likens God to a compassionate parent (Matt 6:9; Ps 103:13). From this tradition, Jesus sees humans as part of a divine household, a family, with its self-giving and loyal love.

Imperial occupation split Judaism into various parties, competing over how best to restore the nation and what shape it should take. The Sadducees put stock in accommodating Rome for Israel's salvation. The Herodians counted upon upholding Herod's dynasty. The proto-Zealots called for rebellion. The Essenes believed in obeying strict purity codes, which the present (profaned) Temple could never do, forcing an alternative one in the desert. The Pharisees pushed priest-like purity on everyone, although they were split over how strict to be. In various degrees, these parties embraced many imperial values, such as aggrandizement, hierarchy, exclusion, and holy war.

Jesus' Jewish vision of a redeemed Israel neither accommodates Rome, nor takes the sword against it. He refuses retreating to the desert and rejects strict purity, ritual, and cultural regulations. His disputes with the other parties, however, were *intra-family*—Jews debating among themselves. Jesus was a Jew. He can never be pitted against the "Jews" as Christians have historically done.

Like all good Jews, Jesus believes in the Mosaic Constitution, which had incorporated the peasant subsistence values. Thus, he intends, "not to abolish the law or the prophets, but fulfill" (Matt 5:17). Israel's early leaders; however, abandoned the Charter in favor of their oppressive privileges. Out of such dire straits rose the *prophetic movement*, the strongest anti-imperial force in human history. Unfortunately, some Christians see the prophets' role as predicting the future, relevant only as their words fit into some end-times scenario. On the contrary, the prophets' primary aim is to critique the elites for *flaunting Israel's safety net subsistence laws*, forewarning them of its dire future consequences. The prophets preserve Israel's faith by interpreting the exile, not as a result of Yahweh's weakness in the face of paganism. Rather, as Isaiah prophesizes, "The Lord enters into judgment with the elders and princes of his people" for taking the "spoil of the poor"—an economic practice that the pagan gods sanctioned (Isa 3:14). The will or reign of God not only prohibits such exploitation, but also demands redress (Neh 5:6–13). When the leaders repent, Israel's exile ends and then it will bless all nations with lasting peace (Isa 2:2–4). Jesus hammers home this same prophetic message in his sayings and parables, most of which, as we shall see, criticize the hard-hearted rich and powerful.

Jesus' own prophetic calling emerges while associating with a contemporary prophet, John the Baptist. Like the prophets of old, John and Jesus proclaim God's imminent reign: "The time is fulfilled, and the kingdom of God has come near; repent and believe in the good news." As John baptizes him, Jesus receives his Spirit-filled prophetic call (Mark 1:9–11, 14–15; Matt 3:2). He will use that mantle to relentlessly call Rome's surrogate leaders and the populist splinter parties to repent from their deeply entrenched imperial values. The flesh and bones of his prophetic message is the "Kingdom of God," a slogan Jesus uses over ninety times and is grounded in the "good news" of subsistence values. As noted earlier, the phrase is best translated "Good Government" or "Good Governing."[1] Following the prophets' lambaste of imperial overstep, Jesus' constant reference to this new form of governing directly counters—and subverts—Caesar's governing. *Nearly all of Jesus' sayings, speeches, and parables are designed as prophetic blasts against the imperial way of life.* The result: like most prophets, including

---

1. Miller, *Jesus Goes to Washington*, 41–50.

John, Jesus is executed, but we are left with a marvelous spiritual/moral legacy.

The trouble begins early when Jesus delivers his inaugural hometown speech and applies Isaiah's prophetic mission to himself: "The Spirit of the Lord is upon me, because he has anointed me . . ." (Luke 4:18–19). After claiming to be a prophet, he references two other prophets, Elijah and Elisha, and delivers an inflammatory prophetic critique of nationalism. In attempting to kill him, the townsfolk confirm his prophetic calling and his fate when he challenges their collective egoism with moral courage. This is why the Philippians hymn describes Jesus as "obedient to the point of death." The prophets were obedient to God's will, to the higher values and callings, even in the face of death. Only persons of extraordinary character possess such rare obedience to prophetic chastening.

To understand the mind/character and mission of Jesus, then, means saturating ourselves in the prophetic books that chronicle blistering denunciations of elite self-serving values along with the prophets' unrelenting calls to repent. Yet, the prophets always spice their critiques with hope. Seeing Jesus within the larger vision of a Jewish prophet allows us to better understand his purposes—to call the nation to repentance and establish his Father's compassionate reign on Earth. Like the prophets, he also seasons his challenges with hope. He is the voice of unrest, while offering "rest" in his divine words (Matt 11:28). As a prophet, Jesus is called not only to crush oppressive values, but also reassemble the shattered world's fragments into a new paradise—humanity's desperate longing.

When we possess his Jewish prophetic mind, our character becomes attuned to hearing the hoarse voice of misery and courageously confronting the American mindset's overstep everywhere—in the home, in the workplace, in government, and around the world. A prophet's silence is sin. Our prophetic call shapes our obedience to serve, exalts Jesus, and brings glory to God's name. The remainder of this work shall explore his prophetic message and the peasant sustainability values upon which it is based; and how they shape our character, the character of our institutions, and bring hope to a Planet wallowing in its waste and reeling in poverty and marginalization. Christians, however, believe not only the message of this fully *human* Jewish peasant/prophet, but also the salvific action of this fully *divine* Lord.

21
The Divine-sovereign Jesus

For Christians, the fully human Jesus is also confessed as fully divine, the sovereign Lord of the Universe, and the unexplainable union of a threesome—The Son on equal footing with The Heavenly Parent and The Holy Spirit. The doctrine of the Trinity is complex. We will not rehash all the issues, except to suggest that Jesus' *full humanity contributes to our appreciation of his divine nature*. In Paul's Philippians passage, Jesus' "equality with God" is affirmed and, ironically, most fully understood in the context of his human incarnation—his humble birth in human form, his extraordinary life of love-filled obedience to God, his compelling mission, and, ironically, his death by imperial forces. How could this be?

An important clue to Jesus' divinity and sovereignty lies in his message about the Kingdom or Good Governing. All emperors claimed to be gods or the children of gods (see 2 Sam 7:14, where God calls King David a son). By calling it *God's* Kingdom, Jesus undercuts the very divine basis of Caesar's reign and his legitimacy to rule. Even more, any hint of Jesus' leadership in this coming new government would assume his divine exaltation, as was the case with all ancient kings. Yet, even more, his divinity stands "above every name"—an open rejection of Caesar's exaltation and claim to divine status (Phil 2:9). Thus, when Christians downplay the Kingdom's political nature, they unwittingly undermine a good case (but not the only case) for Jesus' divinity. What, then, are the implications of a sovereign/divine Jesus?

When Jesus mentions the Kingdom, he means a special kind of governing, not *of Caesar*, but rather *of God*. As we have noted, the Hebrew Scripture equates "God" with the active presence of the "good" (Amos 5:4,

The Divine-sovereign Jesus

6, 14). What Jesus proclaims is the government or governing of the *good*, or the "common good" (of love, justice, and peace). Since these moral qualities are God's essential character, they possess transcendent/universal status. Jesus perfectly embodies God's divine character and fervently displays it everywhere in serving the needs of downtrodden people. After Jesus reads the Isaiah passage, "the Spirit of the Lord is upon me, because he has anointed me to bring good news to the poor . . . ," he makes the Messianic claim that this Scripture is being fulfilled by his presence. (Luke 4:18–21). God has chosen, called, and anointed him, (the meaning of "Messiah"), but also conferred divine power upon him to fulfill his mission. All his titles—Messiah, Child of God, and Child of Humanity—convey both political *and* divine overtones.

When asked at his trial whether he is the "Messiah, the Son of the Blessed One," he responds, "I am; and you shall see the Son of Man seated at the right hand of the Power" (Mark 14:62). Note the subtle, "I Am," the new name for God. God is also called "the Power," bringing attention to God's role in governing through Jesus—the awaited Messiah who compassionately heals and ends poverty and violence (Matt 11:3). This big, powerful, but good government movement led by God's divine Son dwarfs the puny weak Caesar and his imperial claims. Furthermore, because Jesus' values are universal, transcendent, timeless, and robed in majesty, they henceforth subvert all arbitrary imperial ideals that drench the pages of history with blood.

Believing in Jesus' divinity, then, solidifies the universal truth of "do unto others as you would have them do to you," and, consequently, Paul's insistence to regard first the interests of others. Out of his infinitely divine compassion and self-disregarding sacrificial love, Jesus gives up his grasp upon "equality with God" and brings the divine character to Earth and lives it as God would. He comes to serve humanity as a humble "servant" leader in line with the Suffering Servant figure of Isaiah 53. His self-giving and loving "obedience" to his Father proves he is The Child. Thus, God exalts him once again to "equality," as divine Lord and ruler of the cosmos above and against all imperial claims and systems.

Bringing it home, we exalt Jesus and affirm his divinity, not simply by articulating a well-thought-out theology of the Trinity, but when Christ's transcendent character of extreme self-denial takes seed within us and our institutions. We magnify him when we are obedient: to what love tells us to do; to what his teachings demand of us in context; to the reasonable requests others make of us that are within our power to fulfill; and to the obligations and commitments to which we have entered. We exalt him, not in *blind* obedience, but when we confront the arbitrary American "imperial" mindset and act sacrificially on behalf of those who suffer from it. By mirroring Jesus' divine character, we live that transcendent life worthy of the gospel. Yet, how does this godly selflessness shape us as we work for the common good?

22
The Neighbor-serving Jesus

The Philippians hymn sings of Jesus "taking the form of a servant." From this, Paul captures the essence of Christ's character—love's humility that looks to serving one's neighbor. In Galatians, Paul quotes Jesus' love one's neighbor command and then adds, "Through love become slaves of one another" (Gal 5:13–14). This moral ethos was as radical and contrary to the prevailing world view back then as it is with today's Big Me mentality.

In Luke's account, the two great commands to love God and love the neighbor are combined into one command with two parts. This suggests that loving God melds into loving one's neighbor; i.e., neighbor love is not secondary or simply an afterthought (Luke 10:27). When Paul and James refer to Jesus' law of love, they drop the love God part altogether and quote only the neighbor love part. They assume that those who truly love their neighbor will be infused with God's infinite love—a Christ-minded love so extraordinary and powerful that "no one has greater love than this, to lay down one's life for one's friends" (Rom 13:8–10; Gal 5:14; Jas 2:8; John 15:13). John further declares, "Those who love God must love their brothers and sisters also." He bluntly adds the negative side: "Those who say, 'I love God,' and hate their brothers or sisters, are liars" (1 John 4:20).

Neighbor-mindfulness is, then, most sublime, most excellent, most joyful—the quintessential ingredient and chief good of Christian spiritual growth. All meditation, contemplation, and action toward the plight of the neighbor bespeak an elevated Christian character. This Christ-minded love is so unparalled and lofty that Christians adopt a rarely used term "*agape*" to describe it. It is unconditional and unrelenting, even when personally unrewarding. Jesus' exhortation, "love your neighbor as yourself," turns on the logic that we should actually *love others the most*—even more than ourselves—because we naturally love ourselves the most. Then, Jesus can call us to "love one another as I have loved you," which frees us to even "love your enemies" (John 15:12; Matt 5:43–48). Paul's exhortation to sacrificially put our neighbor's interests above our own is simply a restatement of Jesus' emphasis upon the remarkable love command he found in Leviticus 19. Their mantra is, to rephrase JFK's famous saying, "Ask not what others can do for you; ask what you can do for others" (and, of course, this includes "what you can do for your country").

Neighborliness, even to an enemy, is also a national priority as Jesus graphically illustrates in his story occasioned by a lawyer's question, "Who is my neighbor?" (Luke 10:25–37). The two Temple-state bureaucrats are shamed for turning their blind eyes to a badly beaten fellow citizen. Here Jesus encourages all people and governing authorities to provide for their neighbors' basic necessities—needs specifically mirrored in the parable: health care, shelter, and food, even for one's enemies.

Jesus reinforces neighbor love in his story of the hard-hearted-wine-and-dine politician who sneeringly ignores his pitiful neighbor, Lazarus, hunkered at his doorstep, lingering in wretchedness (Luke 16:19–31). He won't even give the starving man a measly crumb that falls from his opulent table. Although this steel-hearted leader does not actively persecute his fellow citizen with anti-loitering, anti-sleeping, anti-panhandling ordinances like many municipalities do today, yet at death he is still whisked from his pride's opulent mansion to languish in Hades. The parable speaks directly to America's calamitous economic state where a few revel in obscene luxury while millions of their neighbors are "food insecure" and grovel in extreme poverty. Here Jesus also undercuts "tricklenomics"—a "crumbs *off* the table" economics—in favor of sharing equally *at* the table that flows with milk and honey. Being unmindful of the neighbor's needs and their equal dignity, either on the individual or corporate level, assures a confirmed reservation in, figuratively, a quite hot, dry place outside of the Beloved Community.

Jesus presses for neighbor-serving love in every sphere of life. We have noted above, his Good Government brings free healing to the ill, free food to the starving, free dignity to the beaten-down, and freedom from all imperial demons that break and crush the human spirit. He reinforces this program in his later campaign speech that contrasts good (sheep) and bad (goat) governing (Matt 25:31–46). While his speech encourages individual Christians to serve others, it is primarily directed toward evaluating

The Neighbor-serving Jesus

governments—their leadership and policies. On the one hand, it describes how good governing provides for the neighbor's basis needs. By providing safety nets for "the least of these" in society, neighbor-mindful governing enters into "eternal life." On the other hand, governing that ignores the needy is "accursed" and sent away "into eternal punishment," the same fate as the granite-hearted aristocrat who brushed aside Lazarus. Yet, Jesus pushes the point further. By scorning government welfare policies, "You did it to me"; i.e., Jesus himself is scorned—harsh words for those leaders today unmindful of their citizens' life-sustaining needs . . . and jarring frankness for those Christians who vote for them. Put positively, a political mindset that looks to the neighbor's need is a mind set on Christ.

Another time, in rebuke of James and John's imperial values and political ambitions, Jesus contrasts good from bad governing, saying, ". . . among the Gentiles those whom they recognize as their rulers lord it over them, and their great ones are tyrants over them. But it is not so among you, but whoever wishes to become great among you must be your servant . . . . For the Son of Humanity came not to be served but to serve . . ." (Mark 10:35–45). By incorporating and emulating Jesus' neighbor-serving character, we become his Kingdom building co-workers to mend our most vulnerable neighbors/citizen's torn safety nets. Then, Jesus is highly exalted, magnified, and glorified above everything else. We best serve our neighbors as compassion- and justice-minded persons, which we will now explore.

23
The Compassionate Jesus

For Jesus, loving God and loving one's neighbor are supreme within Israel's Constitution (Mark 12:29–31). Love is so superior to any other command that Jesus says, "Upon these two commandments hang all the law and prophets" (Matt 22:40). Paul follows by naming love as a fulfilling of the law and calling Christians to hold love as their greatest aim even before faith and hope (Rom 13:8–10; 1 Cor 13:13, 14:1). Later epistles will define God's very character as love (1 John 4:8, 16). Love language, such as "tenderness" and" kindness," dominates the life of Jesus and the lives of the saints.

The term "love," however, is ambiguous. We speak of our love for money, or certain tasty foods, or playing golf. In biblical times, these "lower" self-oriented loves (*eros*) were contrasted with the "higher" self-sacrificing loves (*agape*) directed toward God or others. Throughout history theologians have struggled with the relationship between an acquisitive love and an unconditional self-giving love.

A most important nuance of the higher love is "compassion"—the capacity to identify with the suffering of others, including the passion to relieve their suffering. Compassion plays a cardinal role in the mission of Jesus and why Paul declares it and its cousin sympathy as embodying the character of Christ and constituting the life worthy of his gospel (Phil 2:1–2).

Jesus ushers in a breathtaking spiritual achievement when he reinterprets the most fundamental statute of the Mosaic Charter: "You (meaning Israel) shall be holy, for I the Lord your God am holy" (Lev 19:2). Some of Jesus' opponents believe that holiness results from keeping strict purity

The Compassionate Jesus

laws. Those who ignore these codes are labeled "sinners" and subjected to unbearable persecution, since their non-compliance jeopardizes Israel's restoration and destiny.

Jesus enters the holiness fray by rephrasing the "You shall be holy" command into "Be compassionate, as your Father is compassionate" (Luke 6:36).[1] He makes two monumental changes in the wording—substituting "compassion" for "holy," and "Father" for "God." Both modifications are mutually reinforcing and fundamental to his understanding of Scripture. The image of a parent highlights the compassionate essence of God's character (See Ps 103:13) as also reflected in God's new name, "Yahweh" or "I Am." God, however, does not let the I Am stand alone, but tells Moses "I Am Compassionate, I Am Generous." This "I Am the Compassionate One" knows the sufferings of the people, hears their cries, sees their pains, and then delivers them (Exod 3:7–15, 33:19; Deut 26:7). This radical understanding of God's character as a compassionate and nurturing Father/Parent becomes the reigning theological and moral motif of the law, the prophets, the writings, and of Jesus and Paul.

How we perceive God's character affects our character, though some suggest that how children are raised determines their character and their view of God, politics, and society's role.[2] A strict family model follows a laundry list of rules, metes out physical punishment (spanking) when the rules are broken, shows less affection, and promotes strong self-discipline. Here God is likely to be seen as remote and unapproachable, as wrathful, as easily offended by the slightest infraction, and as punitive and ready to send people to eternal perdition if they do not straighten up. We noted above that God's ire plays a part in Scripture, but it must be seen in the broader biblical perspective—that the compassionate, loving, and nurturing God takes priority and that chastening serves God's loving purposes. God's wrath is temporary, and thus, not God's essence. It sparks when God's compassionate character is under attack by heartless actions toward others. The purpose of God's momentary anger is to tenderize the hard heart.

On the other hand, in a more nurturing family model parents are empathetic to their children's needs; they do not impose arbitrary codes and punish them at the slightest infraction. They especially eschew violence.

---

1. Often translations use "mercy" instead of "compassion." Certainly mercy is a love term, but the usual understanding is that mercy is granted to a wrong-doer and compassion or pity shown toward one victimized. This distinction, however, is not always clear in Scripture.

2. Lakoff, *Moral Politics*, 43–176.

They are open to listen and to discipline in loving gentle ways. They consider their children as deserving the same equal respect and dignity they expect for themselves. These children are more likely to see God as compassionate, gentle, patient, full of mercy and willing to forgive and to forget sin in a blink (see Jer 31:34). This same nurturing character we see in the loving Heavenly Parent, we see in Jesus the Son.

The family image of love is verbalized at humanity's dawn, implied within Cain's question, "Am I my brother's (sister's) keeper?" While Cain's twisted heart answers, "No," the assumed positive response assures that humanity is one large caring family. This seminal truth shapes Israel's religious, moral, and political character. Being one another's keeper and the keeper of the Garden counter the Fall narrative of selfish status seeking, unlimited consumption, and its anger generated savagery. Nevertheless, the "original sin" of selfish pride, which lurks within us all and stamps out any sparks of compassion, inevitably snakes its way into all heartless personal, social, economic, and political arrangements. Yet, Jesus will haunt that original serpent's den and crush his head. In Jesus, the snake has met its mortal foe.

Since pride is the great enemy of compassion, Paul describes Christ's infinite descent as "humbling himself." According to Paul, for us this means, "In humility regard others as better than yourselves." However, with our American mindset, the up-and-coming Big Me is the mantra . . . and our death knell. In humility we realize that we are not self-reliant, but part of the larger community upon which we depend. Humility also undercuts our self-righteousness, forcing us to conclude that we, too, are weak and suffering and in need of deliverance. With humility we live in constant gratitude for what we have received from God and from others, even those flawed others. Humility allows us, then, to enter into the sufferings of others making compassionate service to them possible, a priority, and without demanding a return.

The nurturing and parenting nature of a humble-driven compassion comes through in its Hebrew equivalent: "from the same womb." This image suggests three important truths about compassion. First, the childbirth image speaks to a mother's self-giving pain, analogous to identifying with the suffering of others. Second, parents nurture (nurse) their children so they might flourish and be whole; they think of their children's interests above their own. Third, being of the same womb suggests that every creature is brother and sister, part of one large sharing family called a bio-community. When Jesus calls us to be compassionate like the Heavenly Parent, he is admonishing us to reflect the character of God and consider everyone and everything as family (metaphorically, from the same womb).

Compassion does not make distinctions between good and bad persons, friends and enemies. Jesus says that God is "kind to the grateful and ungrateful" and the Father makes "the sun rise on the evil and on the good and sends rain on the righteous and unrighteous" (Luke 6:35; Matt 6:45). "Love your enemies" means that compassion never looks at another with enmity, but rather as a fellow human being in desperate need of support, especially, the most vulnerable—the voiceless, the helpless, and the defenseless. The compassionate Jesus indiscriminately feeds great multitudes, never separating out the deserving from the undeserving (Matt 9:36). A nurturing God and the nurturing Son bring good tidings to all Creation and meet needs irrespective of nationality, color of skin, religion, species, etc.

Inclusive compassion is the moral of the Good Samaritan story (Luke 10:25–37). The beaten and robbed man is ignored by two fellow Israelites—Temple-state technocrats and surrogates of Rome's compassionless leadership. In contrast, a hated enemy Samaritan "came near him and when he saw him, he was moved with compassion" (reflecting the story line of the "I Am the Compassionate One). Because of his strong character, compassion "moved" him. He provides the victim medical treatment, transports him to shelter for recovery, and pays the bill until he can stand on his own. Unlike the Temple-state that ignores a brother in need, the Samaritan treats him like a literal brother. As his brother's keeper, he fulfills the peasant ethic and the Constitutional mandate to meet immediate and long range needs. In exhorting the Temple-state scribe who occasioned the parable to "go and do likewise," Jesus trumpets compassionate governing that impartially provides a safety net until those hurting completely recover.

In Jesus' Parable of the Prodigal Son, household compassion reigns even toward those gone astray due to their own bad decisions (Luke 15:11–32). When the pig-tending "unclean" son returns home, the father, "filled with compassion, ran and put his arms around him and kissed him." Here again compassion results in action, even when the unimaginable happens—the father (representing God) hugs and kisses his son and *renders himself unclean*.[3] For Jesus, solidarity with others greatly outweighs heartless purity codes.

---

3. See Miller, *Jesus Goes to Washington*, 77–81 for a discussion of this parable and its civic implications.

Jesus not only *feels* compassion, he *acts* compassionately to right the wrongs of persons and structures. He understands the reasons for misery. He once looks out on a huge crowd with compassion and describes them as sheep without a shepherd, a biblical image of failed leadership (Matt 9:36, 14:14–21 with Ezek 34:1–10). This broadside against the present leaders castigates them for not only ignoring the people's plight, but actually causing it. Jesus steps up as a compassionate person of action to heal them without pay and when the disciples want to send the people away so they can buy food, he replies, "They need not go away, you give them something to eat." His free feeding of thousands points to the ancient manna provisions during Israel's wilderness wanderings and carries political significance, confirmed by the twelve baskets left over (referencing the tribes of Israel). It also fulfills the dawning Good Government promise of a "land flowing with milk and honey," where health care for the sick and food for the hungry are free.

Jesus commissions us and our institutions to model the very character of the compassionate Heavenly Parent with its family and household implications. Unfortunately, the individualism that feeds the American Dream tightly caps our deep inborn wells of compassion. The imperial value system, with its acceptance of large gaps in social standing and wealth distribution, extinguishes flickers of compassion and then castigates those victimized. Nevertheless, when Jesus refers to an unrepentant rich man, he says, "for God all things are possible" (Matt 19:26). He assures us that God can instill a softhearted character trait so we might naturally identify with the downtrodden and bring appropriate relief. The self-emptying person, then, is the person filled with the compassionate character of Christ and walks worthy of his Gospel. A big heart exalts the Jesus of boundless love, but a love wedded to justice.

24
The Justice-minded Jesus

Compassion, as the highest neighbor-serving virtue, is not simply a personal response to personal suffering, but also a *public* action that changes unloving social, economic, and political structures. We have noted that the love-neighbor command Jesus quotes is from Israel's Constitution and directed to the nation (Mark 12:29–31; Lev 19:18). When love enters the civic sphere, it immediately partners with justice to find broader solutions to human misery. Compassion gives justice its heart, while justice gives compassion its direction. When either languishes, they both languish.

For instance, it is commendable to serve dinners to our houseless friends and neighbors. However, it is also important to confront the broader injustices surrounding poverty; to push municipalities to provide extremely low income and supportive housing as a human right; to advocate for the elimination of Jim Crow type "nuisance laws" that deprive people of places to sleep and to fundraise on street corners. Compassionate justice calls out slurs and stereotypes. It advocates for the civil rights of despised and marginalized people. It refuses to allow prejudices to be called "solutions."

"Justice" is primarily a political/legal term. Only the state metes out justice through law (although the broader notion of fairness should govern all our personal dealings). As noted above, any Christian call for biblical justice thrusts one into the political, social, economic, and ecological battles raging today. On the opposite side, those Christians who say "Christians or the church should not become involved in politics," imply that Christianity has nothing to do with biblical justice. However, to be true to Jesus, believers and congregations should not only be involved, but their role may be

PART 2—EXALTING JESUS

to present alternatives or mediate the battles; or even take sides as Jesus did. Yet, they should never push religious-specific views within the political realm.

Justice harbors the idea of fair and equal treatment in giving one their due. It conveys three fundamental notions: (1) retribution for crimes committed; (2) distribution of resources; and (3) the rectifying of past harms or inequities. We need to know which aspect of justice is being addressed in any given biblical text. Often God's justice is read as retribution, when the actual meaning points to distribution of goods or compensation for past injustices. Even after knowing which form of justice is meant in a text, the *scope* of justice is highly debated. For instance, what is the proper and just punishment for capital crimes, what is a fair way to distribute resources in society, and how should people or groups be compensated for past injustices?

Some scholars now suggest that the biblical term "righteousness" should in many instances be translated "distributive justice," as when Jesus says, "Strive for the Kingdom of God and its distributive justice, and all these things (food and clothes) will be given to you as well" (Matt 6:33). Can you imagine how Evangelicalism might have been reshaped if we had read its signature verse as, "All scripture is inspired by God and is useful for teaching, for reproof, for correction, and *for training in justice*" (2 Tim 3:16, italics mine)? Justice is mentioned hundreds of times in the Bible, and thus, a word from the mouth of God—a *divine* word. Many Evangelicals now acknowledge the big "hole" they have left in the gospel and speak more compassionately about social, economic, and ecological justice issues.

Jesus enters the debate following the lead of the prophets. He speaks of retributive justice or "eternal punishment" for social callousness. On distributive justice, he insists that the rich must "sell what you have and give the money to the poor." On compensatory justice, he looks to a great reversal in which the "last" economically and socially will be "first," i.e., those pushed to the bottom will be brought up (Matt 20:16, 25:46; Mark 10:21).

Jesus brings justice to the streets and is particularly outraged at the injustices that Galilean peasants must endure. His dawning of the Good Governing will bring about the great reversals, while mending the shredded subsistence safety net. The reversal motif is dramatized in Mary's Magnificat—the powerful are brought down, the lowly will be lifted up, the hungry filled, and the rich sent away hungry (Luke 1:46–56). Jesus drives home these upheavals in his Beatitudes sayings: "Blessed are you who are

The Justice-minded Jesus

poor, for yours is the Kingdom of God. Blessed are you who are hungry now, for you will be filled." Then Jesus turns the table on the rich "for you have received your consolation," and "you who are full now, . . . will be hungry" (Luke 6:20–25). For Jesus, compensatory and distributive economic justice and its life-sustaining benefits are owed the poor and hungry, while retributive justice awaits the callous rich. Today, Jesus would be accused of creating class warfare. Yet, how God must see red as the rich get richer, while the poor languish in poverty.

According to Jesus, love and justice go hand in hand and both serve the other. The most important law, the Golden Rule, inherently links compassion and justice (equality). First, to treat another as you want to be treated implies that both are on an equal footing. Second, the rule implies empathy by walking in the other's shoes and bearing their suffering. Third, love makes justice *generous*, since loving others is modelled upon loving ourselves whom we always treat most generously. We shall look first at Jesus' special treatment of the *socially* "humbled" (the shamed) and then his equalizing program for the *economically* "last" (the desperately poor).

Jesus lives in a strict honor system divided between wealthy male leaders possessing most of the honor (dignity) while everyone else bears shame. His constant reminder that the humble shamed will be exalted constitutes a frontal assault upon the inequalities within the honor culture. His reversal statements decree justice and dignity to all human beings, whatever their lot in life, ethnicity, religion, illness, age, class, gender, sexual orientation, housing status, or nationality.

For Jesus, privilege is always destructive to those unprivileged and so he intervenes on behalf of women, who are tradition-bound and languish in shame and lowliness, only a step higher than a slave. Countering some cultural warriors, he exonerates a woman about to be executed for her behavior: "Neither do I condemn you . . ." (John 8:3–11). He turns his world upside down by memorializing a courageous woman who lovingly breaks male protocol. He scolds the men and demands they "leave her alone" (Matt 26:13). He is so committed to the dignity of women that he surrenders his own honor by allowing a woman to shame him, and then commends her, "Woman, great is your faith" (Matt 15:21–28). Surprisingly, he publically converses with and honors a despised Samaritan woman by requesting, "Give me a drink" (John 4:7–26). Yet, even more, he dignifies lowly prostitutes, claiming they "will go into the Kingdom" ahead of some well-positioned religious leaders (Matt 21:3). Jesus continually lifts up women and considers it a great injustice that they lack equality. It's no surprise that so many women followed him around (Luke 8:1–3). When "the least of these" (including woman) are exalted, Jesus is exalted.

Regarding compassionate economic justice, Jesus tells a heartfelt story about some unemployed laborers (Matt 19:30—20:16). Being a "Good Government is like" parable, it speaks directly to enacted economic policies. Jesus begins (and ends) the parable with his "first/last, last/first" reversal saying, so his listeners will immediately anticipate a fundamental challenge to the unjust imperial economy. A vineyard owner hires a group of laborers early in the morning and then at other times of the day, sending them into his fields and telling them, "I will pay you what is right." Some work only one hour. Unexpectedly, he pays every worker the same—enough to feed their food insecure families for the day. The all-day workers, having born the burden of the scorching sun, are outraged, believing they deserve more. However, the landowner (depicting God and good governing) holds to the peasant economic justice that guarantees subsistence in the meanest of times (as day laborers then faced). Compassionate justice dictates that breadwinners are owed a "living wage" so their families will avoid starvation, no matter how much or little they produce. The parable speaks of a generous government's rectifying justice or affirmative action, providing a safety net for those underemployed and living at the economic margins.

In our individualistic, all-day, meritocratic culture, we might find it hard to swallow that one-hour workers are paid the same as the twelve-hour ones. Our Americanized values are not in tune with Jesus and Paul's compensating ideals, although we fully understand and affirm the first/last equalizing principle when professional sports teams draft players. As one respected economist writes, "Looking out for the other guy, isn't just good for the soul—it's good for business."[1] The landowner's generosity is not charity, but a mark of a governing compassion-laden justice that flies in the face of American go-it-alone competitive values.

In his famous prayer, Jesus also references laborers who lack bread to feed their families (Matt 6:9–13). After we pray, "Your kingdom come . . . on earth," we petition God to "give us this day our daily bread," or bread that sustains for the day. This now translates to breadwinners asking, "Give us this day a living wage" (and not just a minimum wage). Generous justice's special consideration institutes policies that neither snatches bread nor substitutes stones for it, but ensures every citizen the basic necessities

---

1. Surowiecki, "Why the Rich," 34, where he quotes Joseph Stiglitz.

The Justice-minded Jesus

to live a respectful and decent life, which Jesus reinforces in his Judgment of the Nations speech (Matthew 25).

Early on, Christians pooled their money, considering it a spiritual ideal of their Kingdom assemblies (Acts 2:43–47, 4:32–37). When the early church commissions Paul to go to the Gentiles, their *only* request was that Paul remember the poor, to which he replies, "I was eager to do" (Gal 2:10). For Paul, the more affluent assemblies are "privileged" to redistribute their wealth for "fair balance," even if it burdens them. In fact, Paul here defines "grace" as economic generosity and that this redistribution of wealth is a sure test of love's genuineness and one's obedience to the gospel. Paul models this generosity after Christ's self-emptying: "who was rich, but for your sakes he become poor, so that by his poverty, you might become rich," an unabashedly economic application of the Kenosis hymn (2 Cor 8:13–15).

Given the persisting gaps between rich and poor today, Jesus' equalizing first/last principle, Paul's fair-balancing economics, and the early church's Kingdom practices are still compelling. Thus, justice-minded Christians will joyfully promote wealth redistribution through a living wage, higher taxes on the rich, inheritance reform, entitlements, a more democratic economic system, and other polices designed to bridge the persistent and widening chasm between the rich and poor, even when these economic policies press upon them personally.

We Christians, with vestiges of Adam's original sin, are constantly tempted to grasp after divine-like superiority and fulfill our greedy impulses, ready to rear their heads in moments of weakness. Christians possessing the Justice-minded Jesus bring honor to the shamed and equality to the downtrodden as *second* nature, exactly like our Heavenly Parent who impartially "sends rain on the righteous and the unrighteous" (Matt 5:45). They will affirm the American ideals of freedom and justice "for all," but will always be ready to level a prophetic blast when the American mindset limits or distorts those values. They will join with Native Americans, African Americans, women, Latinos, the working and out-of-work poor, the houseless, LBGTQs, and other minorities in their ongoing justice battles. Christians who have the same justice-minded character as Jesus will live the worthy Christian life. In so doing, we exalt Jesus and celebrate him as the Lord over our social, economic, ecological, and political decisions.

25
The Welcoming Jesus

History's most horrendous inequalities and injustices have been committed against those who do not look or act like the dominant society. Collective egoism and its inevitable social distancing is the basis for all prejudice and bigotry. The resulting discrimination against minority groups has taken a ghastly toll. Margaret Mead, the famous anthropologist, observed that regardless of the stated reasons why groups form, the underlying purpose is to exclude those dissimilar and considered inferior.[1] For instance, I am a Baptist. If pressed, I would give reasons why being a Baptist is a smidgen better than being a Methodist or Lutheran, or a Catholic. Of course, persons in the latter groups give reasons why their affiliation is at least a fraction or so better than being a Baptist. Unfortunately, this superior/inferior dynamic is the fertile seedbed of intolerance.

Intolerance is grounded in an ancient value system which considered differences in nationality, birth, status, gender, sexual orientation, age, etc., as criteria for assigning honor or shame. Historically, Christianity's hands have been splattered with the blood of out-grouped peoples. In my lifetime, Christian Fundamentalism has reinforced racism, genderism, anti-Semitism, anti-immigrationism, heterosexism, Islamophobia, nationalism, climate denialism, and classism. The social logic of unchecked intolerance leads to labeling people who are different as misfits, and in the worst case, as contaminants to be excluded from the community. The next step in a tragic social logic is to eliminate out-groups (genocide) as we saw in Germany and more recently in East Africa, Eastern Europe, and Charlotte, North

---

1. Mead, *Blackberry Winter*, 100–105.

The Welcoming Jesus

Carolina.[2] Intolerant theologies, often espoused by well-known Christian groups and their leaders, now saturate the airwaves and pulpits.[3]

Jesus shows remarkable tolerance toward the socially marginalized. He reaches out to an ostracized man plagued by a skin disease, declaring, "Be made clean." He defends eating with the hated tax collectors and "sinners" with "I have come to call not the righteous but sinners" (Mark 1:40, 2:15). Another takeaway from his first hometown campaign speech is his prophetic challenge to the popular cultural prejudice that God showers blessings upon Israel, while cursing outsiders and enemy nations (Luke 4:16–30). So opposed is Jesus to intolerance that he considers "anyone who slurs his brother or sister" a murderer (Matt 5:22). He turns a Samaritan considered bad into a good Samaritan because he fulfills the most holy command in Israel's Constitution by compassionately helping a dying enemy (Luke 10:25–37).

Christianity bears heavy responsibility for discriminating against homosexuals. Some Christians refuse to acknowledge the full rights of GLBTQs, more specifically, the right to marry. It's heartwarming; however, that some Christian leaders have repented and asked forgiveness for their previous prejudiced attitudes. Many now speak positively about homosexuality and consider it no different than being left- or right-handed.[4]

In a National Book Award winning work, *Homosexuality, Christianity and Social Intolerance,* the author examines the questionable biblical texts and the Christian attitude toward homosexuals.[5] He notes that early Christianity did *not* condemn homosexuality; in fact, some of its leaders may have been homosexual. In a later book, he examines a number of early Christian homosexual marriage rituals, undermining the falsehood that Christians have always believed marriage is between a man and a woman.[6] Moreover, he points out that around the thirteenth century the same social and political factors that led to the shameful anti-Muslim Crusades, the Inquisition, and anti-Semitism also gave rise to Christian anti-homosexual attitudes. After that disastrous time, Christians searched diligently for the

---

2. Kelsey, *Racism*, 96

3. *Truth in History* broadcast, Feb. 7, 2016 where tolerance, diversity, pluralism and feminism were decried.

4. Gushee, "Reconciling Evangelical Christianity," 148–54.

5. Boswell, *Christianity, Homosexuality*, 91–117.

6. Boswell, *Same-sex Unions*, 162–261.

few remote biblical texts they could twist to justify their already pre-existing prejudice.[7]

These few Bible verses (the six "clobber passages") that some use to justify their negative attitudes, actually have little bearing on homosexuality *per se*. Some texts actually speak to male cult prostitution (Lev 18:22 with 1 Cor 6:9; 1 Tim 1:10). Another addresses shameful acts of male to male viciousness and the flaunting of *customary* (not "natural") social relationships (not "sexual relations") between women (Rom 1:26–27; see 1 Cor 11:14 where "nature" means "customary"). Genesis 19, the Sodom and Gomorrah story, and its parallel in Judges 19 are preceded by remarkable acts of hospitality. Just as Abraham meticulously entertains the messengers, so also the father-in-law and the old man are overly hospitable to the Levite and his concubine. Ironically, the true message of Genesis and Judges is not God's anger over homosexual behavior, but anger over the lack of hospitality shown the stranger; i.e., those who happen to act "strangely" or differently, *which today includes homosexuals*. Ezekiel defines the "sin of Sodom" as having pride and excess of food and not caring for the poor and needy (Ezek 16:49). Jesus also interprets the demise of Sodom and Gomorrah as judgment upon those who "will not welcome you" (Matt 10:14–15). Being unhospitable to homosexuality remains a dark splotch on Christianity and commends rebuke in the spirit of Jesus.

As noted before, the Bible's own principles of interpretation demand that all verses hang upon the law of love. Thus, the six obscure passages can never be directed toward cursing this minority group. During my youth, divorce was virtually looked upon as an unpardonable sin. Today it is hardly ever mentioned in family value debates, even though Jesus was quite clear, taken literally, that divorce and remarriage was adultery. I could find 30 verses in the Bible that clearly justify slavery, yet no Christian would literally follow them today except for the most die-hearted racist who still rallies for the "curse of Ham." The Spirit of loving justice and the context of ancient practice (that divorce was a male franchise for serial marriages and that emancipatory slavery was a humanitarian alternative to killing prisoners of war) must guide our interpretation and application of such texts. Thus, even if there exists only one verse that seems to condemn homosexuality as we know it today (none actually exist); we must search for its true meaning under the scrutiny of the Golden Rule/love-your-neighbor principles.

---

7. Boswell, *Christianity, Homosexuality*, 269–302.

What homosexuals fear most is that Fundamentalists will apply a Bible verse that calls for the death penalty when men lay together, even though this law actually addresses male religious prostitution and not homosexuality per se (Lev 18:22, 20:13). This has contributed to an atmosphere of violence that shrouds homosexual relationships. Some Evangelicals have exported their hateful views and been blamed for Uganda's strict laws to incarcerate homosexuals and possibly subject them to the death penalty. As recently as 2015, someone threatened to introduce a California ballot measure that advocated executing homosexuals.[8]

Many Evangelicals would deny gays and lesbians the right to marry based upon the Creation story, which they believe defines marriage as between a man and a woman. The focus in Genesis; however, is not upon their *biological differences*, although they are different, but rather upon their *moral relationship*—their "oneness" or community, resulting from humanity being created "in the image of God" (Gen 1:27). When Jesus quotes Genesis in the divorce debate, he comments exclusively upon the "oneness" part: "What God as joined together, let no one separate" (Mark 10:9). What is morally normative for him is not biology, but a loving relationship. For this reason, he redefines "family" as "whoever does the will of my Father in heaven," rejecting biology (lineage) as decisive for faith and morality (Matt 12:50).

The greatest threat to marriage today is not LGBTQs, but husbands who lord it over their wives. Is it not time for Bible-believing Christians to come to their senses, shed their putrid prejudices, come home to the way of Jesus, ask forgiveness, affirm homosexuality as a birth/right gift of God, and bless same-sex marriages as they do heterosexual ones? An exalted Jesus demands such; a person of character will do so.

Furthermore, while the church traditionally *described* marriage as that between man and woman, it never *defined* marriage as such. The church defined it with the famous 3 Rs: the Remedy for our desires (Paul's negative directive to marry rather than burn with desire); the Raising of children; and the Relationship of love. Today we hold more positive attitudes about sexual desire and emphasize the *proper* raising of children. However, given Jesus' primacy of love, the loving relationship element must float to the top and govern the other two Rs. This *moral* priority of defining marriage compels the Christian community of character to welcome LGBTQs with open arms and be honored to participate in their holy matrimony.

---

8. Calnewsroom, 1.

Another marginalized people in America are those going through hard times and ending up houseless. They have either slipped down to the economic ladder's last rung, or they have fallen off the ladder completely. The Great Recession has swelled their ranks, and reading the stories of struggling families on the road to ruin, plummeting through the shredded social safety net, is alarming and heart-rending. Being labeled "homeless" lands one in a minority group that faces social scorn at every corner, subjected to name-calling and slurs like "transient," "vagrant," "bum," "hobo," "tramp," "panhandler," "drifter," "derelict," "drunkard," and other demeaning epitaphs. They are often likened to nuisance and "foul" animals and "annoying mosquitoes," considered an "infestation" and contagion.[9]

The houseless are victimized by Americanized values such as self-reliance and hard work. These result in petty and onerous discriminatory Jim Crow ordinances that criminalize sleeping in public places or in cars, loitering, asking for food or funds, etc.—all designed to torment those at the economic bottom. The fear of our brothers and sisters, and the resulting disdain, is the sin of "homelessphobia," guaranteeing their exclusion and persecution. Thus, they are refugees in a merciless society, virtually exiled in their own land, considered a scourge and treated as disposable, as dross.

With such negative attitudes and discriminatory laws, the risk of our friends without homes dying on the streets rises dramatically. Their daily humiliations and frustrations become so intense that they often reach a boiling point, and the lid blows. Rather than providing safety nets, society casts out dragnets, hauling them off to jail, strapping them with a criminal record, and making it even harder to get work and housing. We cannot imagine the heavy psychological and physical toll this vicious downward cycle takes. No wonder some go through a mental crisis and are driven to find relief in drink and drugs. I poetically summarize this tragedy as follows:

> *A Tale of the Unknown*
> The person nearby in scruffy rags,
> Crouched with scrawled cardboard,
> Gleaning slim charity for scanty food.
> You might, if human, notice him, but not see—
> Not see her contained sorrow
> In pale cheeks, in hollow eyes.
> Not see his hope and his burden: just to be.

---

9. Alcorn, "Bummed out," editorial.

The Welcoming Jesus

> Who knows the reasons:
> Born of a mother in poverty?
> A father's mean switch?
> The law's stern stare?
> A war's savage scene?
> A balm of poison?
> Unimaginable loss, unspeakable rejection?
> Harmed in a million ways.
> Who knows . . . who cares?

Jesus understands bigotry quite well. At birth there was no room in the inn. From childhood he knows rejection and ridicule, given the scandalous circumstances surrounding Mary's pregnancy. When his father and protector Joseph dies, he is forced to leave home, experiencing houselessness first-hand with "nowhere to lay his head" (Matt 8:20). Out of desperation, he joins his ascetic cousin, John the Baptist, the leader of a houseless group, disenchanted by the present religio-politics. Given his own experience and his Father's love, Jesus holds a special place in his heart for the "highway and back alley" people (Luke 14:23). He knows the pain of social rejection—a person looked upon as unclean roadside trash, given no respite from ridicule, and where snide remarks are the norm. His descent from heaven was not only humiliating, but infinitely humiliating.

A Christ-like character breaks the trance that keeps us persecuting others and from learning to love them more deeply and broadly. When we Christians show reasoned tolerance to marginalized people, whether of color, or of a differing faith, or nationality, or gender, or housing status, we magnify Jesus and further confirm his Lordship over our lives and over the nations. We also increase the likelihood that others will confess him and bend a knee to him as one who loves all people and who breaches the thick walls that divide us and frees all those held captive in the deep dungeons of discrimination.

26
The Spirit-of-the-law Jesus

Compassion, justice, and welcoming languish until they are codified into good laws that enhance every citizen's life-chances. Contrary to popular opinion, Jesus firmly believes in law and is, like us, committed to his Constitution, although, as with the prophets, he believes it needs renewing (Jer 31:31–34). During the famous Transfiguration event, in the presence of Moses the lawgiver and Elijah the prophet, God tells the disciples: "listen" to Jesus; confirming that he is now the new prophet/lawgiver (Mark 9:2–8). Thus, Jesus stands squarely within the Jewish legal tradition and is aware that judicial injustices crush the masses. He states it forthrightly, "Do not think I have come to abolish the law or prophets. I have come . . . to fulfill" (Matt 5:17–18). But what did he mean by "fulfill?"

When asked about the most important legal statute, Jesus quotes the "love God/love neighbor" statutes from his Constitution (Deut 6:4; Lev 19:18; Mark 12:29–31). As noted before, by leading with, "Hear, 'O Israel . . . ,'" he confirms that these are primarily national laws and not simply personal moral norms. In Matthew, the Gospel most concerned about the law, Jesus adds a most important addendum—upon these two laws "hang all the law and prophets," a phrase he also adds to the Golden Rule, a close cousin of the "love your neighbor" law (Matt 22:40; 7:12).

These laws of loving justice, then, are not only the supreme *legal/moral commands*, but they also act as the ultimate *criteria for legal interpretation*. They bring to light the law's inner, intended meaning—they act as a law's "Supreme Court," so to speak. For Jesus, then, his coming to "fulfill" the law means he interprets every statute in light of God's character and expressed purpose—for compassionate justice to reign throughout Earth. Paul calls

The Spirit-of-the-law Jesus

this the *spirit* of the law that gives life, as opposed to the *letter* that brings death (2 Cor 3:6). Because loving justice is universal, it reaches forward to interpret our civil laws today.

Since the phrase "law and prophets" is shorthand for the Hebrew Scripture as a whole, in the mind of Jesus *loving justice is the hermeneutical (interpretative) principle for every verse in Scripture, and thus, the determining factor for biblical authority.* Every Christian must implant this same Jesus mindset when approaching Scripture as the Red Letter movement suggests. The implication: no verse in the Bible can be understood in an unloving way, no matter what it seems to read on the surface. Simply quoting a verse is never sufficient to establish its authority. We become *profoundly* biblical when we decipher a text in light of the Bible's own authoritative principle of interpretation—loving justice. Of course, we become *extraordinarily* biblical when we sacrificially act upon the text's love-filled interpretation in our social, economic, political, and ecological lives.

A marvelous model for a non-literal interpretation is found in the Bible itself. If asked to define "fasting," we would probably give the stock answer, "the discipline of abstaining from food." Yet, look at how Isaiah redefines fasting: "to loose the bonds of injustice . . . to share your bread with the hungry . . . to bring the homeless poor into your house . . . to cover the naked" (Isa 58:6–7). A traditionalist might badger Isaiah, "How dare you change the plain meaning of Scripture!" However, given the notorious injustices at the time, Isaiah applies love's interpretive maxim to expand fasting's common usage in order to launch a broadside against the elite's rampant feasting off the backs of the poor. He confirms the enduring truth here that *every* practice, ritual, and word of the inspired Scripture must pass the love and justice test, otherwise we misapply them. Put negatively, any interpretation of a biblical word, phrase, or practice that perpetuates social and economic injustice is wrong. Take slavery. This heinous practice is *biblically, morally, and legally* wrong period, no matter how some literal interpretations of the Bible were used by slave holders to justify it. Slavery is an egregious violation of the Golden Rule/love your neighbor law that governs the meaning of *every* text that speaks of slavery.

Jesus himself interprets the Hebrew Scripture from the higher standpoint of compassionate justice. The Fifth Commandment requires that we honor our parents. Previously we mentioned an onerous special interest law called "Corban" in which dedicating one's wealth to the Temple releases that person from supporting their aging, needy parents (Mark 7:9–13).

Taken literally, the Fifth Commandment does not specifically compel children to underwrite their elderly parents. However, the commandment's inner morality of compassionate justice demands it. As interpretive principle, the Golden Rule mandates that when you were young and vulnerable, your parents cared for you; now when they are old and vulnerable, fairness demands you must provide for them. Corban violates love's equal exchange, making a travesty of family responsibility. Jesus is so outraged by this heartless literalism that he draws upon another Hebrew law: "Whoever curses father and mother must surely die." Corban is so heinous that Jesus considers it a curse upon one's parents, and thus, deserves the severest punishment.

Other examples from the Ten Commandments confirm Jesus' rejection of literal interpretations of law and Scripture. The sin of adultery is not simply the act of infidelity (although it includes that), but also "whosoever looks upon a woman with lust" (Matt 5:27–28). No one considered "bird-dogging" an act of adultery. Jesus' deeper understanding of adultery; however, covers those first covetous desires to use another for one's pleasure and the subsequent philandering. So also murder, a grievous crime, means more than taking another's life. It also includes those degrading acts that lead to murder such as being "angry with a brother or sister," or "if you insult a brother or sister," or if you say, "You fool." Rage, ethnic slurs, and disrespect are destructive to community, and thus, are liable to judicial penalty (Matt 5:21–22).

Jesus' New Constitution subjects the established laws to love's renewal in changing situations. Laws are not written on stone, but remain alive—to be "fulfilled" when facing new challenges. Consequently, in the mind of Jesus, legal rights and their attendant duties are always expanding, a truth for today. Look at the movements for greater civil rights even in my lifetime: for African Americans, for women, for Latinos, for the differently-abled, for farmworkers and other undocumented workers, for Native Americans, for homosexuals, and for the emerging rights of the houseless. To possess Christ-mindfulness is to embrace his way of interpreting our Constitution and the Bible—his way of plowing new ground with love's justice so that everyone flourishes.

For your reflection: what if all our church rituals were interpreted in the way Isaiah redefines fasting? If true fasting means "feeding the hungry" and "bringing the homeless poor into your house," then could we not say the same for true prayer, true Bible reading, true tithing, true baptism, and

The Spirit-of-the-law Jesus

true praise? Possibly Isaiah might redefine the Lord's Supper as making sure every poor person is "food secure," especially in light of the overfed rich in America. Actually, this is precisely what Paul means in chastising the Corinthian assembly for eating all the communion food, while "the have-nots" starve (1 Cor 11:20–22). Certainly baptism points toward "total immersion" (I am Baptist) into these moral concerns. This Christ-minded hermeneutic of "religious ritual," then, would surely end hunger, houselessness, and other social crises in America and beyond. When we possess Jesus' character and interpret laws, Scripture, and traditional practices in ways that advance loving fairness in the personal and public realms, we exalt Jesus who inspires good laws that serve all equally and that everyone is more likely to respect and obey.

27
The Non-materialist Jesus

Our world spews out new products and gadgets at an unimaginable pace. We are daily bombarded with thousands of messages to buy this or that to be happy, successful, and important. Products are not just conveniences or objects to satisfy our cravings, but definers of what it means to be human in a material consumer-oriented world. The relative worth of material items indicates our own self-worth and dignity. Lodged deep in the American psyche is the dream not just to keep up with the Joneses, but to surpass them. Our conspicuous consumption—our endless purchasing to impress others—condemns us to a buying-and-selling mentality where everything is up for barter. For this, we constantly search out more and more storage space.

This perspective insidiously creeps into Christianity, reinforced by the Prosperity Gospel. With little moral squeamishness, Christians drive expensive cars, live in high-priced mansions, dine at top-notch restaurants, and vacation at posh resorts. In fact, they consider these normal and justified, even assuring themselves that, "God has really blessed us." In standards of economic lifestyle, Christians differ little from their upscale non-Christian neighbors. I am as guilty as the next of a sumptuous lifestyle.

Jesus tells it straight, "Take care! Be on your guard against all kinds of greed; for one's life does not consist in the abundance of possessions" (Luke 12:15). If ever a saying of Jesus rebukes the American materialistic mindset, this is it. For Jesus, it boils down to "all kinds of greed," which we face everywhere, in every institution, in our economic structures, and deep in our hearts. We are never content with just enough; we crave abundance. To then illustrate his point, Jesus tells about a rich man who has so much he cannot store it all. So he builds bigger and bigger barns and reassures his soul, "Soul, you have ample goods laid up for many years; relax, eat, drink, be merry." The man seems fully satisfied, but God considers his life meaningless and "demands it." All that hoarding only brings him an early death. In his near death experience, he hears only, "You fool!" and "The things you have prepared, whose will they be?" Jesus leaves us Americans with this inconvenient question about wealth's distribution—implying that our greedy grasping and stockpiling contribute nothing but harm to ourselves, to our community, and to our Planet. Greed is one of the seven deadly sins and why Jesus tries to show us that life is more than what we own. By ignoring these truths, what fools we become.

Jesus' harshness toward wealth is illustrated by the rich political leader who asks him how to "gain" eternal life, another way of inquiring about entering God's Kingdom (Luke 18:18–30). Of course, questions of gain were always on the minds of the wealthy, which is how they define their spirituality (like prosperity preachers do today). While the rich man's piety embraces most of the Ten Commandments, his impiety selectively ignores the laws about coveting and also "stealing," especially from the poor. More importantly, all the commandments submit to the most important law—to love the neighbor in need. In this man's case, greed triumphs and he is left outside the Good Government, confirming Jesus' truth that it does not profit "to gain the whole world at the price of one's soul" (Mark 8:36, Phi).

Paul also speaks of "gain," but how he may "gain Christ." Gaining Christ means the "loss of all things" and regarding them as but dung (Phil 3:8). Few of us would consider all our possessions as a pile of human waste. Worse, Christians whose "minds are set on earthly things" and whose "god is the belly," Paul calls, "enemies of the cross of Christ" (Phil 3:18–19). For some Christians belly-filling materialism is their "god," the content of their character—at enmity with Christ. What an apt critique of Christians today who worship at the altar of the American Dream.

Responding to the rich ruler's question, Jesus speaks fiercely in the name of redistributing scare resources: "Sell all that you own and distribute the money to the poor." The man is predictably perplexed and resistant. Loss of wealth means loss of honor and political power which rich and positioned persons never give up easily, even if it means trading on their eternal destiny. This encounter occasions Jesus' famous hyperbole on the difficulty of a rich person inheriting the Kingdom: "It is easier for a camel to go through the eye of a needle than for a rich person to become a part of the coming Good Governing" (Luke 18:25). In answering his stunned disciples' question about who then can enter, Jesus allows for one exception—when God does the seemingly impossible and softens hard hearts so they give back even more money than they have extracted as Zacchaeus does. Because of this tax collector's willingness to redistribute his wealth, Jesus assures him, "Today salvation has come to this house" (Luke 19:9).

These two accounts also subtly reflect the peasant and Jesus' view that accumulating wealth in the midst of misery is a sign of extreme selfishness, the lack of compassion for those suffering, and a violation of subsistence principles. Wealth is a form thievery—a sin—and why the wealthy must return the money *for their salvation*. Knowing that evil always beguiles, Jesus shows great compassion for the rich man, but has little sympathy for the lifestyle that holds him captive, although the man endures his chains willingly. Jesus considers it a calamity that some wallow snout-deep in luxury while others reach vainly for a handhold as they plunge down the pit of economic disaster. His message remains relevant given the present growing chasm between rich and poor in America and the world.

Money in the ancient world was round, silver, and gold, replicating the moon and sun, and thus, objects of worship. For Jesus money is a false god and insists, "You cannot serve God and wealth (Mammon)"; it's a form of idolatry (Luke 6:13). We examined Jesus' parable about an aristocrat who "feasted sumptuously," but whose worship of riches so blinded him to the need right at his doorstep that he ends up in hell (Luke 16:19–31). The aristocrat's affluence is the dream of many Americans today, even though billions starve and the future of the Planet demands the path of sustainability. Jesus compels us to be content with necessities and not swim in wasteful luxuries, especially as an ever expanding world population vies for limited resources. It's high time that churches seriously proclaim breaking our ties to Mammon and live with bare necessities, called by some a "minimalist" lifestyle. The Earth Charter calls for "material sufficiency," which ought to become a Christian marker of the gospel-worthy life that exalts the Jesus who renounces extravagance.

Tragically, our drive to possess more and more dulls our feelings of compassion and sidetracks our sense of justice. Do we believe Jesus, when he says, "Where your treasure is, there your heart will be also" (Luke 12:34)? His comments on money, wealth, and consumption are easily ignored or explained away by those of us who revel in "compulsive consumerism," as Pope Francis names it.[1] American Christians often claim that wealth is not a sin, only the *love* of money. Back then, as now, wealth in the midst of poverty implies our deep love for and idolatrous worship of money. In addition, the sin is compounded because poverty *results from* wealth accumulated by the few. The rich generally have and always will fight attempts to redistribute their wealth, unless through charity. However, recent studies show that relatively little (about 15 percent) ends up directly helping the poor. Most charity in America goes mainly to keep institutional churches afloat, while the rest supports education, the arts, etc.[2] Besides requiring the rich politicians to eliminate poverty through redistribution, Jesus redirects the practices of almsgiving and tithing toward "justice" for the poor (Luke 11:41–43). For Jesus and for us, charity never substitutes for economic justice, except during the interim.

Will we continue to bow our knee and worship at a shrine of "economic growth" that opposes a more equitable distribution of wealth (through progressive taxation or expanding entitlement programs)? Christ's simple-living character also compels us to honor Creation by curtailing our use of the Planet's resources and reducing our carbon footprint. For the followers of Jesus, the American Dream no longer permits living in luxury, but rather points to everyone receiving an equal sustainable piece of a limited pie. When our moral character looks to meeting the basic needs of others and not our own accumulation of things, we bow to, confess, and exalt the Non-materialist Jesus.

---

1. Francis, *Laudato Si'*, 133.
2. The Center, "Patterns," 30.

28
The Forgiving Jesus

The word that best describes the character and mission of Jesus is "giving." He opposes a system based upon "taking" grounded in imperial values. Jesus views God's character as generous, expressed by the word "grace"—a term that propelled the Protestant Reformation. God's graciousness brings us salvation through the death of Jesus, even though unmerited. Simply stated, God's grace is God's generous forgiveness poured out upon humanity, which then spurs us to be generously forgiving toward others, even those we think "undeserving."

Since giving, in all its ramifications, infuses the character of God, then *for*giving, too, comprises God's essence and becomes central to Christian character. To forgive means to "give up" one's anger, resentment, and revenge for wrongs done. Forgiveness implies that people inevitably make mistakes and harm others. One way to help mitigate the harm and reduce escalating violence is for perpetrators of injustices to humbly ask forgiveness, which also includes attempts to amend. Yet, for Jesus, forgiveness reaches even to those wrong-doers not seeking it, an unheard of notion in his time.

Jesus lives in an honor culture where slight insults could escalate into family feuds and violent retributions, lasting for centuries, like the Hatfields vs. McCoys. Due to Rome's occupation, people were routinely shamed by losing their Land and means of survival, having to struggle for any strand of dignity. Thus, Jesus exhorts people to "give over" their honor protocols and never extract revenge. Thus, "If anyone strikes you on the right cheek, turn the other also; and if anyone wants to sue you and take your coat, give your cloak as well; and if anyone forces you to go one mile, go also

The Forgiving Jesus

the second mile. Give to everyone who begs from you, and do not refuse anyone who wants to borrow from you." (Matt 5:40–43). These "acts" of forgiveness were especially remarkable, but relevant, in volatile villages under unbearable stress.

When asked how often to forgive, Jesus' exhorts, "seventy times seven" (Matt 18:22, seven being the number of completion). For Jesus, life is an exercise in forgiveness. People can only live in relative harmony when forgiveness and mercy prevail. Those in long and successful marriages know this, although continual forgiveness never justifies staying in abusive relationships—those that, I might say, disproportionately affect women.

God's generous giving and forgiving also addresses the common retort, "I can forgive, but I can't forget." Certainly those who have experienced great harm and unimaginable evils cannot and often will not forget. However, a remarkable passage in Jeremiah (also the longest Hebrew scriptural text quoted in the New Testament) speaks of a new vision and a new Constitution in which God says, "I will *remember their (Israel's) sins no more*" (Jer 31:34; Heb 8:12, italics mine). Given the Christian belief in God's omniscience, this passage is quite remarkable. Could it be that the all-knowing God could actually forget something? Yet, when it comes to remembering sins, God chooses a flawed memory. Furthermore, God removes our sins as far as East is from West; i.e., even, metaphorically, out of God's infinite sight (Ps 103:12).

Forgiveness then is unconditional. Look again at the Prodigal Son story, where the son sins so grievously against his father (representing God). Without judgement, without waiting for an explanation, but "while he was still a far off, his father saw him and was filled with compassion; he ran and put his arms around him and kissed him." "Then," after this total acceptance, does the son confess, "I have sinned against heaven and before you" (Luke 15:20–21). This same unconditional forgiveness is the main story line of Victor Hugo's *Les Miserables*. Jean Valjean repays a priest's kindness by stealing some abbey silverware. After he is caught and brought back, the priest covers for him by implying that the stolen silver was a gift. In fact, the priest hands him another candlestick. This breathtaking act of forgiveness transforms Valjean's life. Yes, love does "cover a multitude of sins" (1 Pet 4:8).

Now we understand Jesus' last words on the cross, "Father, forgive them for they know not what they do." The reference to "them," of course, is not the Jews, but the imperial forces that put him to death because he was subverting their values. Yet, by forgiving them, Jesus gives his executioners a ready-made exoneration—*their unawareness of what they were doing*. Modelling our lives after Jesus, we too are ready to forgive, to forget, and even ungrudgingly to search for exonerating reasons why someone has wronged us. Possibly that person, too, is a victim of larger negative social forces.

A major plank of the Lord's Prayer is, "Forgive us our debts as we also have forgiven our debtors" (Matt 6:12). The petition is structured in such a way that receiving forgiveness is predicated on our forgiving others—the same reciprocality expressed in the Golden Rule and the love neighbor commands. Our willingness to forgive others is now recognized by psychologists as a prerequisite for our own mental health. When childhood (mostly family) injustices accumulate, victims later attempt to rebalance the ledger by being unjust toward others (mostly toward their own innocent children and why abuse tends to be intergenerational). Healing begins when we articulate reasons to forgive (exonerate) others, partly by realizing that they, too, were likely innocent victims of ledger-balancing family injustices.[1] In other words, they too, "did not know what they were doing." Even further, Jesus demands, "do good to those who hate you, bless those who curse you, pray for those who abuse you" (Luke 6:27–28). The word "those" highlights a forgiveness that is not just individual, but also reaches out to groups, including other nations. Jesus forgives Rome's injustice to him when we might expect him to exact revenge.

Living a life of forgiveness means cutting others slack and being slow to judge and condemn. Using hyperbole, Jesus exhorts, "Why do you see the speck in your neighbor's eye, but do not notice the log in your own eye?" (Matt 7:3). When we acknowledge our own failings we are quicker to forgive the shortcomings of others, allowing families and communities to thrive. For example, Christians who quickly forgive are uneasy with the death penalty and push for rehabilitation. When prisoners have served their time, Christian forgiveness supports reintegration into society and the possibility of restoring their God-given rights, like voting and opportunities to compete equally for jobs.

Forgiveness, however, does not sanction passivity. It stands strong in face of injustice and attempts to right the ongoing wrongs people have endured such as why a disproportion of prisoners are minorities and why

---

1. Krasner and Boszormenyi-Nagy, *Between Given and Take*, 12–16.

they are targeted by law enforcement. Forgiveness seeks transparency and change, whether personal or social.

The forgiveness of debts in The Lord's Prayer points not only to sins or trespasses, but also references economic indebtedness (a use of "forgive" even today). During bad years, the peasants barely survived and were often forced to eat the next year's crop seeds, sending them into an inescapable debt spiral. The elite were quick to foreclose. As Jesus' Prayer assures, when God's good government comes on Earth, all debts will be cancelled and the ancestral plots returned as originally legislated by the Sabbath debt forgiveness and Jubilee policies outlined in the Mosaic Charter. For Jesus, to "forgive our debtors" assures "daily bread." Jesus reinforces debt forgiveness in his exhortation, "do not refuse anyone who wants to borrow from you," and further, "expect nothing in return" (Matt 5:42; Luke 6:35). This remarkable economic forgiveness in Jesus' Kingdom plan is a "hard saying" for most Americans because of our self-aggrandizing capitalist mindset.

Jesus was a generous person and forgiveness infused his daily walk. Having his same mind/character means generously giving up our anger and revenge and living the worthy-life of forgiveness. This Christ-like character may seem extremely difficult as we navigate through the social wreckage left by heartless personal actions and malignant political policies. We glorify Jesus when we consider forgiveness as both a personal and Good Governing virtue. It wipes slates clean and takes up the cause of those affected by incarceration, loan sharks, badly written mortgages, and excessive interest payments. We exalt the forgiving Jesus when we reject knee-jerk retaliation and approach every negotiating table with both a forgiving character and acknowledging the need to be forgiven.

29
The Truth-seeking Jesus

A comprehensive study on lying and truth telling reported that most people lie and stretch the truth on a fairly regular basis. Distressingly, they most likely lie to loved ones.[1] All the forms of lying—spins, half-truths, perjuries, the fine print, exaggerations, white lies—weave their way through the fabric of everyday life. All the commercials we see in the media bombard us with little deceptions that chip away at our respect for truth. We now live in a "post-truth" world that accepts "alternative facts" as reality.

Furthermore, our gullibility is breathtaking and charlatans always lurk, ready to pounce and bleed the unsuspecting dry with some lie, confirming the truth that behind every falsehood is a hidden price tag. Unfortunately, some Christians, given their trusting nature, are susceptible to slick, pocket-lining, flimflam artists whose half-truths prey upon innate selfish-driven fears. Dishonesty, however, refers not only to our everyday dealings with others, but also enters into the realm of ideas. Aristotle claims that *intellectual* dishonesty is as wrong as a bold-faced lie. So truth must always prevail, even if it counters a cherished belief.

A most popular saying of Jesus is, "I am the way, the truth, and the life" (John 14:6). The word "way" is significant since it becomes the name of the early Christian movement (Acts 9:2). The Jesus way; however, is the way of "truth"—the unalloyed truth that percolates into every realm of human experience, edges out all shades of falsehood, and ultimately brings and sustains "life." Jesus provides an end to humanity's night of ignorance and deception, along with its bed partner—evil. Yet, truth and knowledge

---

1. Patterson and Kim, *The Day America*, 48.

The Truth-seeking Jesus

in Scripture also imply an intimate relationship with some object and makes uninterrupted roundtrips between the heart (feeling) and the mind (reason).

That Jesus declares himself as the "truth," compels Christians to be forthright in our daily dealings. Truth telling was mandated in the Ten Commandments—do not bear false witness. Jesus insists upon speaking the truth in his famous saying, "Let your word be 'Yes, Yes' or 'No, No'" (Matt 5:37). Mean what you say and do not spin your pledges, statements, or answers for selfish reasons. This includes disclosing pertinent information that someone fails to notice, like the used car salesman who responds to a disgruntled buyer, "You did not ask me about the transmission." Possibly most dishonesty thrives upon what is left unsaid.

Due to the power of sin, deception always holds sway over the truth, and why we must rely upon a higher power. How disheartening, then, that the assault upon truth often marches under the banner of Christianity. Religious quacks infiltrate churches and mine the airwaves for easy pickings, appealing to the lowest human denominators—false fear, self-centeredness, guilt, emotionalism, and the endless repetition of stock phrases. Their guarantee of extravagant promises and manifold blessings (under the claim, "God spoke to me") exploits every spiritual and psychological gimmick. Like the sweepstakes pitches that flood the mail, they especially prey upon the poor and elderly.

Since the Hebrew Scripture celebrates wisdom as divine essence, the Bible classifies a group of books as "Wisdom." Wisdom preserves justice and goodness; saves us from the path of evil; is more precious than jewels; and by it God created Earth (Prov 1:20—3:20). In these books, the wise person is continually contrasted with the fool. Jesus, too, has little patience for foolishness and stupidity.

He commends a scribe for answering "wisely" regarding the great commandments to love God and neighbor, assuring him, "You are not far from the kingdom of God" (Mark 12:34). He tells parables about greed's folly when one ignores the truth that "life does not consist in the abundance of possessions" (Luke 12:15–20). Some foolish virgins do not wisely think ahead and "keep awake," thereby missing God's Kingdom (Matt 25:2). Jesus holds not only the common titles of prophet, priest, and king, but also that of wise man. Paul refers to Jesus as the "wisdom of God" (1 Cor 1:24, 30).

We also tarnish our Jesus who is truth when we foolishly deny the most basic findings of science. Historically, Christianity has opposed scientific truth when it seemed to conflict with long held and cherished beliefs. It took centuries for the Catholic Church to acknowledge that Earth is not the center of the Universe. Darwin still shakes the foundation of many Christians who reject evolution. As noted before, most Christians who attend church weekly believe that humans were created in their present form within the last 10,000 years, shrugging off the whole scientific enterprise.

We concede, however, that science is a double-edged sword. It has not only made life better for many, but it has also produced weapons of mass destruction and the technology to exploit Earth's resources, both of which threaten life's future sustainability.[2] All human endeavors need to be subject to higher moral truth. Yet, Christians must be open to new insights from the scientific method for the sake of integrity and to make life better for everyone.

Christians are called to distinguish good science from "junk science," especially when harmful effects are at stake. For instance, the anti-vaccination movement has duped some believers into refusing to immunize their children. Vaccinations are truly a miracle of modern medicine and have added at least thirty years to the average American's life expectancy. Their links to autism and other diseases have been largely discredited. Many base their views on unproven antidotes and the common logical fallacy *post hoc ergo propter hoc* (after this; therefore, the cause of this). It is like those who claim they acquired the flu right after receiving a flu shot, not seeing this as coincidental bad timing, since, for most, the medicine takes about two weeks to become fully effective.

The vaccination issue brings home Jesus' Golden Rule and Paul's admonition to consider the interests of others above one's own. Scientists recognize that containing certain diseases is based upon "herd immunity"—that every family takes its responsibility in protecting the whole community. When families, looking to their own interests, refuse to vaccinate, they harm, not only their own children, but also put at risk other children—as the measles outbreak at Disneyland confirmed. When children are harmed, Jesus shows no patience: "It would be better for you if a great millstone were fastened around your neck and you are drowned in the depth of the sea" (Matt 18:6). No medical or religious basis for jeopardizing the health of your child and other children can ever exist and is why a Jehovah Witness

---

2. Francis, *Laudato Si'*, 69–78, claims the "technocratic paradigm" causes our ecological crisis.

who refuses a lifesaving blood transfusion for their child should be charged with child endangerment.

The more we appreciate the advances of science and understand the mind-blowing dynamics of astrophysics, the intricacies of matter at its most elementary levels, and the amazing workings of the human body, the more we praise the omniscience and awesomeness of God. By affirming and prizing the remarkable laws of God within Nature, we reverence the Creator of those laws. Stated negatively, to flaunt, ignore, and despise God's laws of Nature which science is always unfolding, is like holding all God's laws in contempt, including God's moral laws. It desecrates the One we claim to love. And when those laws potentially endanger humans and Planet, God has, thankfully, given us the minds to try to mitigate them.

How we approach the Bible also reflects a character of integrity. Christians claim, and rightly so, that their beliefs stem from the Bible and its authority. The Bible, however, is basically a moral/spiritual book intending to teach us how to live God-like lives and how we should treat one another. Its purpose is not to provide lessons in geology or paleontology. Given that Jesus is the truth and that he values the human mind and its wisdom, one should approach Scripture in a reasonable way and not play the fool in how to use it. This means examining texts in their broader historical, political, sociological, and religious contexts to better understand the intended meanings back then.

By adopting valid methods of interpretation, we reduce the likelihood of mistakenly using biblical texts under the false guise of "this is what the Spirit told me." Yes, the Holy Spirit interprets texts, but not in a mindless vacuum. The Spirit inspires the lifelong work of scholars who have immersed themselves in the first-century world, learning its languages and cultures, and always subjecting their work to rigorous peer critique. Their labors should not be dismissed out of hand. It is intellectually dishonest to do so—an assault upon truth and the one who is truth. We betray biblical truth by demeaning their scientific research and its results.

The scientific method, then, while not perfect, is a necessary starting gate for understanding what the Bible is saying to us today. People need to question pastors and televangelists who, with seemingly little respect for the truth, speak off the top of their heads on every biblical or scientific topic. Many of the more recently formed Evangelical Churches demand very little formal or professionally accredited training for their ministers. If someone were about to face life-threatening heart surgery, would we not expect the surgeon to have undergone rigorous medical school training, to have been supervised by recognized professionals, to have passed comprehensive exams, to be licensed and subject to boards of review, and to keep up on the best medical research? If anyone practiced medicine without the above criteria, we would consider that person a quack. Yet, some will entrust their spiritual hearts to a religious leader without rigorous training and professional safeguards. Often, the only criterion of a good minister is personal charisma, regardless of their love for and dedication to truth.

Thus, we magnify Jesus when we love him, not just with our heart, soul, and strength, but also with our mind. We love him when we develop a love for our never-ending learning about him and all his Creation; we love him when we love the laws of Nature; we love him when we critically evaluate any idea passed off as truth, including the views in this book, many of which are controversial and subject to respectful debate; and we love him when we appreciate good peer-reviewed biblical scholarship. This is how we all grow into the truth and how we pay majestic tribute to Jesus whose way is truth and life. When we say, "It's the gospel truth," we claim a character of integrity worthy of Christ's gospel. By enthroning truth, we enthrone Jesus.

30
The Peace-loving Jesus

Since Cain, kin kills kin. By announcing Jesus' birth to the peasant shepherds, the angels herald a long lost peace on Earth. This peace gladdens hearts mired in hopelessness due to the constant fear of Rome's violence (Luke 2:14). True, Rome claims to be the harbinger of peace, proclaiming *Pax Romana*, but its peace is a slash and stab, blood-spattering, and conquering-at-will peace. Those who dare challenge Roman rule are subject to execution, and a most torturous one—crucifixion. Hanging on a cross was a visible media event designed to strike terror in the population and quench potential dissent. Death is agonizingly slow; the body is left to rot and be torn apart and devoured by animals of prey. Crucifixion stood as heavy vengeance and a sadistic way to keep the peace.

The Roman cross also symbolizes a structural brutality that seeped into every level of society, infusing policies that appropriate family lands and enslave people, rape their daughters, and draft their sons to fight in wars of conquest. Even Roman entertainment, such as the gladiator "games," reinforces and satiates bloodlust. Jesus introduces a different form of governing, not a peace based upon violent suppression, fear, and bribery, but a peace grounded in loving justice.

Shalom (peace) is a fundamental value of the Judeo-Christian faith. In Judaism it describes the very character of the community and continues as a most treasured gift to humanity. While now a common greeting among Jews, it conveys more than "hello," or simply the absence of conflict. More positively, shalom includes the total health and well-being of individuals and community. Jeremiah speaks about the "welfare (shalom) of the city" and "in its welfare you will find your welfare" (Jer 29:7). Note here that an individual's welfare is linked to the community's welfare. In fact, shalom is tied to all social values: without justice there is no peace; without security there is no peace; without sufficient food and shelter there is no peace; without everyone prospering there is no peace; without freedom from oppressive structures there is no peace; without good health there is no peace; without a productive Land there is no peace. The Bible's expansive view of peace assumes that the individual and the community will flourish in every way.

Swayed by American individualism, Christians often limit biblical peace to inner tranquility. The "peace of God, which surpasses all understanding" (Phil 4:7) is usually interpreted as purely psychological. Certainly, inner peace is an important dimension of peace, given the turmoil and anxiety that nearly every person experiences in a turbulent world. Jesus assures his followers, "Peace I leave with you; my peace I give unto you. I do not give to you as the world gives. Let not your hearts be troubled, and do not let them be afraid" (John 14:27). At another time, he says, "Do not worry about your life . . ." (Matt 6:25). Yet, does Jesus see peace as only inward?

For Jesus, the peace that assures inner tranquility also reaches into the social and political sphere and assumes both the elimination of structural violence and the promotion of national well-being. Jesus, a beneficiary of the Prince of Peace title in the Hebrew Scripture, is forthright on the issue of peace and political violence. In the preamble to his new Constitution, he gives special honor to the peace*makers*, calling them the "children (or offspring) of God." This contrasts with Caesar's claim to be a child of the gods, who is only a peace*keeper* "as the world gives"—a peace undergirded by waging butchery and brutal suppression. Jesus instructs his itinerant disciples, "Say peace to this house" (Luke 10:6). Here peace conveys its broader meaning of general welfare or as we call it today, "the common good." Like a good community organizer, he counters imperialism by restructuring village life around revived subsistence values that heed the community's peace or well-being (Matt 10:7–8).

Like the prophets of old, Jesus puts little hope in military might as expressed in his well-known saying, "For all who take the sword will perish by the sword" (Matt 26:52; see Hos 3:18; Jer 9:23–24). This admonition counters both Rome's systemic violence and that of the rural resistance directed against Rome. Contrary to popular works that portray Jesus as a zealot who concedes to physical force, Jesus believes in the "soft power" of

The Peace-loving Jesus

persuasion and more subtle "hidden" forms of resistance through stories (parables), honor challenges, and criticism of the rituals and customs that perpetuate dominance. For this, he would experience "enhanced interrogation," leaving his *body* drenched in blood, but never his *name*.

Furthermore, Jesus rejects the eye for eye, tooth for tooth retaliation law and insists, "Do not resist evil," and, "If anyone strikes you on the right cheek, turn the other also," and "Love your enemy." These are the strongest statements for reducing the tsunami of violence ever recorded in human history (Matt 5:38–44). Revenge, the expected response for even the smallest slight, is unthinkable for Jesus. The only acceptable "retaliation" is to "do good to those who hate you, bless those who curse you, pray for those who abuse you" (Luke 6:27). Jesus understands that fulfilling human need, essential for interpersonal, community, and international relationships, defuses "enemyness" and is the first step in promoting both inner and political peace.

As a man of peace, yet a resister to Rome's oppression, Jesus exorcises demons as another way of engaging political power. Once he meets a man with a host of demons, called "Legion," which unambiguously references the devastating physical and mental effects of Rome's rule (Mark 5:1–20). That the tortured man is forced to live in the village cemetery with chains he continually breaks, illustrates the unleashing of Rome's brutal and deadly power. Jesus casts the demons into a herd (a military term) of unclean pigs which march (another military reference) into the sea. His exorcism subtly rebukes Rome's contaminating presence, and envisions the day when its Legions will be cast out of the Land and back into the sea from whence they originally sailed. The clamor that calls the many to war is silenced. Not only will Rome's demise usher in true peace—shalom's healing—but it also testifies to "what compassion the Lord has shown."

In a world shot through and through with perennial wars, a humble peacemaking character (beyond simply peacekeeping) must infuse Christ-minded Christians. This world that wallows in violence has left most of us its victims in some form: whether bullied as a child, abused in the home, sexually or physically assaulted, having an acquaintance gunned down, or having fought in wars, and on and on. When we add up the mayhem, maybe violence really is as American as apple pie. Our fixation upon guns is a case in point.

In America, as many firearms exist as people. Our frontier mindset sanctifies guns to the point of worship, with some seemingly placing more trust in guns than in God. The prophet Jeremiah decries those who trust in swords and chariots (Jer 9:23). Hosea graphically and chillingly describes the results of such trust: "bloodshed follows bloodshed" (Hos 4:2). The Zechariah prophecy, tied to Jesus' ride into Jerusalem, predicts, "He will cut off the chariot from Ephraim and the war horse from Jerusalem; and the battle bow shall be cut off, and he shall command peace to the nations (Zech 9:10 with Matt 21:5). Jesus' "triumphal entry" on a lowly donkey signals God's triumph over all weapons. We magnify Jesus when we refuse to tolerate the ongoing bloodshed due to the easy access to guns and when we work diligently to "cut off" all armaments.

Nevertheless, we live in a sin contaminated world. Thus, nations are forced to follow Just War criteria to quell violence by bellicose countries or berserk gunmen. However, to glorify Jesus, Christians will critique any misuse of Just War principles, while working to eliminate all arms races, all weapons of mass destruction, and all cues and means of violence such as guns. To wantonly justify force and the threat of force is the work of hell and belittles Jesus. It mocks the meaning of events surrounding his birth and death such as the angels' announcement of peace, Herod's slaughter of the innocents, and Jesus' gruesome crucifixion.

Jesus also speaks forthrightly to the issue of family violence. We noted above that some Christians embrace a "tough-love" approach, reflecting the strict parent model. They sometimes justify corporal punishment with the verse that speaks of sparing the rod and hating (often misquoted as "spoiling") the child. The parallel second half of the verse admonishes those who love their children to discipline them, but not with physical punishment (Prov 13:24). Rather, the "rod" could refer to a shepherding rod, not used to hit the sheep, but to guide them. Also the rod may refer to a piece of wood with some carved commandments that a child wears as a necklace. To spare the rod of guidance/teachings would certainly do a child great harm. Harm also comes to a child when hit, even under the euphemism of "spanking."

Studies show that harsh physical discipline in childhood contributes to greater juvenile delinquency, substance abuse, and mental health problems.[1] Spanking has been shown to be generally ineffective in changing behavior, and, as noted in Part 1, actually teaches children it's OK to be violent toward others. Some more progressive countries have outlawed corporal punishment and many states have banned it in schools. It bears repeating that Jesus honors children and decries anyone "harming one of these little

---

1. Fergusson and Lynskey, "Physical Punishment/maltreatment," 617–30.

ones" (Matt 18:6). By rejecting both physical and psychological violence toward children, we possess Christ's character and we magnify his name.

Women are especially vulnerable to abuse and its violence, an enduring human scandal. We already examined how husbands can mistreat wives. Jesus also addresses the plight of women in other social contexts. The woman who crashes the all-male party to "perform a good service" to Jesus is victimized by male wrath and possibly their violence. Jesus steps in and rebukes them, "Let her alone; why do you trouble her?" (Mark 14:3–9). May Jesus' "let her alone" echo to our time as the war on women never ceases.

Jesus quells male violence when he takes the side of a woman singled out for her part in an act of adultery: "Let anyone among you who is without sin be the first to throw a stone at her." He exonerates her and gently exhorts her, "Neither do I condemn you. Go your way, and from now on do not sin again" (John 8:1–11). Another time he condemns men who "look upon a woman with lust," confirming that women are not the means to male use or abuse (Matt 5:28). He protects women by declaring that divorce laws were written for males "because of the hardness of your hearts" (towards women). He warns men that "anyone who divorces his wife and (as a result) marries another commits adultery" (Matt 19:8; Luke 16:18).

Jesus believes that humanity has true peace within its grasp, not a peace created and sustained by violence or its threat, but a peace grounded in his main message of compassionate justice. A person characterized as a peacemaker strives to understand and accept differences, an essential precondition in serving others. Peacemakers at every level and dimension of human existence, from the inner psyche to the international, fulfill his birth announcement: "Peace on Earth." He is then magnified as the true Prince of Peace.

31
The Union-of-nations Jesus

As we have suggested, the life worthy of Christ's gospel that compels us to humbly consider others better than ourselves, challenges not only individual selfishness, but also the collective egoism that governs nations. Certainly, love of county or patriotism is a worthy virtue, but can easily degenerate into moral blindness. American Exceptionalism assumes a superiority complex that translates into imperial-like clout over countries not bowing to our national interests. We are constantly reminded of American's Manifest Destiny due to our nation being founded upon Christian principles and that God has bestowed upon us a special place—"a city upon a hill." Nationalistic fervor often rides the wave of religious fervor.

That America was established upon Christian principles does sound a ring of truth. This nation emerged with a belief in justice, freedom, and well-being for all. In practice, however, these values primarily benefited white male property owners. This "value gap" runs counter to the biblical traditions. The prophets apply these values to all peoples and nations regardless of standing. They form the basis of a general philosophical ethic that undergirds Jesus' Golden Rule—the principle of equal treatment that transcends national borders.[1] Christians, in their desire to possess a Christ-like, Spirit-filled character are highly motivated to pursue justice, freedom, and well-being as universal values that apply to everyone and every nation alike.

---

1. Gewirth, *Human Rights*, 128–41.

The Union-of-nations Jesus

One renowned scholar claims that every one of Jesus' references to the Kingdom conveys an international flavor.[2] Jesus yearns to end Israel's internal exile and occupation and revive Israel's original destiny—*to be a blessing to the families of Earth* (Gen 12:3). Actually, this is God's goal for all nations, so that Egypt is called "my people," and Assyria "the work of my hand" and they both become "a blessing in the midst of the earth" (Isa 19:24–25). In line with the prophets, Jesus courts the belief that Israel's restoration would convert Gentile rulers who normally "lord it over" their citizens into "like one who serves" (Luke 22:25–27). Thus, God will bless nations (and judge them), not based upon manifest destiny, but upon whether they provide life sustaining safety nets for their most vulnerable citizens (Matt 25:31–46).

Another truth that emerges from Jesus' inaugural Nazareth sermon is the ungodliness of blind patriotism (Luke 4:16–30). Jesus challenges the townsfolk's popular theology that God blesses only the Israelites, while God brings woe to other nations. In a dramatic reversal and with some creative interpretation, Jesus says, "There were many widows in Israel in the time of Elijah . . . and there was a severe famine over all the land; yet Elijah was sent to none of them except to a widow at Zarephath in Sidon." This alone offends the villagers, but he does not let up: "There were also many lepers in Israel during the time of Elisha, and none of them were cleansed except Naaman the Syrian." That God favors a Gentile woman and an enemy general *in lieu of* suffering Israelites, repudiates their blind nationalism, and sparks their collective rage. Like the prophets of old, Jesus proclaims internationalism. Like the prophets of old, Jesus faces death because no prophet with international mindfulness is "accepted in the prophet's hometown."

Following in the footsteps of Elijah and Elisha, Jesus heals a hated Samaritan whose "faith has made you whole," and the daughter of a Gentile woman whom he allows to best him in an honor duel, commending her, "Woman great is your faith! Let it be done to you as you wish" (Luke 17:19; Matt 15:28). In his famous parable, the enemy Samaritan embodies international compassion by helping a dying Israelite. Jesus gives God's favor to a Roman Centurion by declaring, "In no one in Israel have I found such faith." This occasions his most powerful statement on internationalism: "I tell you, many shall come from east and west and will eat with Abraham and Isaac and Jacob in the kingdom of heaven" (Matt 8:5–13). Like Caesar's rule, the Good Governing that Jesus brings reaches to every nation, but, unlike Caesar, Jesus invites the scorned to a banquet of equals where they

---

2. Jeremias, *Jesus' Promise*, 70.

feast on dignity, true justice, peace, and well-being—all grounded in God's grassroots compassionate justice.

God-fearing Christians not only dream that Jesus' hopeful prediction of all nations being united will come quickly, but will also work overtime to realize it. Unfortunately, some Christians, seduced by America's sense of superiority, are cold to international cooperation and reject bodies like the United Nations and their moral protocols (the Universal Declaration of Human Rights, the World Court, and The Earth Charter). Some with a distorted eschatology even consider such alliances as the Antichrist's one world government scheme. Ironically, it is very "Antichrist" for Christians *not* to see themselves as citizens of the world community first and then of their particular countries—what Jesus unrelentingly teaches about true patriotism.

One symbolic way Christians might ratify Jesus' internationalism and his Lordship over all peoples is to fly the United Nations flag in their sanctuaries rather than the American flag. Jesus is magnified, glorified, and esteemed when our faith and our walk are in tune with his absolute commitment to the nations united under the values that sustain communities and usher in universal shalom. This international cooperation is especially important in our ever-shrinking world with its unrelenting poverty, its weapons of mass destruction, its violent extremism, and its deteriorating ecosystems.

After 2000 years, Jesus' vision has emerged with the birth of the United Nations and the increased cooperation of countries to solve world problems. International bodies enhance his dream that all nations be united as one family sharing equally at a common table. However, this international sentiment that played a major role within Jesus' alternative Kingdom (Government) led to his crucifixion. When we reject the unity of and respect for nations, we ignore and disrespect Jesus. Yet more, as illustrated by the murderous response to his Nazareth speech, extreme nationalism kills Jesus anew and leaves a withered moral character in its wake. We adopt his prophetic character by critiquing a blind collective egoism that spins a nation's glaring flaws. We exalt him by affirming cooperation among the union of nations and by promoting reasoned diversity and mutual interests.

32
The Creation-care Jesus

Earth is in the throes of death. The Planet is going to pot because of humanity's mindlessness and denial of responsibility. For the Christ-minded, care for the environment must become a priority for the gospel-worthy life. After all, we believe that God created Earth and called it good; and from its "dust" (out of its minerals and processes) humans were "brought forth." God named humans (linked to "humus"; i.e., soil) "Adam" (derived from 'adhamah meaning "Earth"), providing divine confirmation of our physical pedigree to the Planet. God guided Earth's history and showered it with a unique blend of elements as the building blocks of all animals, minerals, and vegetables. Given these marvels, Christians believe that Creation declares the glory of God (Ps 19:1). Indeed, the more scientists learn about Earth; the more poets praise it; the more artists describe it; the more we are in wonder of its intricacy, complexity and beauty; the more we are in awe of its majestic Creator and its Lord—Jesus.

Unfortunately, some Christians have little regard for preserving Earth, whether because their theology is more heaven oriented, or their eschatology predicts Earth's demise anyway so why bother, or they align with the denial groups that tend to demean science. Or they may interpret the Genesis passage about "subduing" Earth as a mandate to exploit Creation, and thus, the right of private property owners to extract resources at will. Consequently, Nature is gradually being disrobed of its glory and of its testament to God's goodness. At the heart of our disregarding Earth lurks the pull of the American way of life—its insatiable consumption with its vomited waste.

PART 2—EXALTING JESUS

We have suggested elsewhere that Jesus embraced an ethic of material sufficiency mediated by his peasant background. These values were grounded in the peoples' high regard for the Land that found their way into their Scripture beginning with Genesis. Jesus was familiar with Genesis and draws important moral insights "from the beginning of creation" (Mark 10:6, where he criticizes serial marriages).

The first three chapters of Genesis undergird a viable Earth ethic and its sustainability principles, which intone Jesus' Kingdom message. First, God speaks Earth into being, and thus, God remains its owner and preserver; we are but its tenants, commissioned to steward it for the good of all.

Second, God's Earth is ordered out of chaos, governed by the divine-infused laws of Nature, and arranged according to the "days" of creation. These days represent a sequencing of the necessary ingredients for a finely tuned ecosystem: light, air, land, water, life, and the decay essential for sustaining life.

Third, God commissions humans to upkeep Earth's habitats, to enjoy its fruits, and assign creatures their name (naming being God's way of conferring dignity and respectful treatment).

Fourth, God places limits upon our unlimited desires to take from Earth, symbolized by the forbidden tree at the Garden's center.

Fifth, because of our selfish push to hoard Earth's resources (taking whatever is a delight to our eyes) and our arrogant drive to be equal with God, humans flaunt God's command, resulting in "The Fall."

Sixth, because of Adam's "original sin," humans become Nature's outcasts, resulting in paradise lost. We become enemies of Earth and ultimately of one another resulting in brother killing brother. This part of the Genesis story tells the dark side of human history and the origins of imperial values that have devastated people and Land to the present. Following the storyline of Cain and Abel, Jesus tells a parable about a vineyard's selfish imperial tenants who commit murder rather than share Earth's bounty. In God's good time they come to a fateful end and the owner will "give the vineyard to others"—to the peasant farmers so they can sustain their families (Luke 20:9–19).

Seventh, humans need a savior who will redeem us and change our character from selfish killing instincts and values to other-serving values so we will "keep" Garden Earth, it habitats and inhabitants, and become our brother and sisters' "keeper"—preserving communities and ecosystems into the far future.

The Creation-care Jesus

Yet, it remains disheartening that in the face of Genesis and the overwhelming scientific consensus, many Christians are caviler about preserving God's good Earth. They unwittingly provide religious cover for the greed and bottom lines of a corporate America that exploits Earth's benefits, while using it as a garbage dump. We are dangerously reaching, or have reached, the "tipping points" of no return for many forms of global pollution. Our sustaining Garden is crying out because we grievously and selfishly ignore or downplay the Creator God's command to restrain our material urges. We will ultimately lose the resource extraction and pollution-generating battles with Earth and with God, made worse by the resulting wars that humans fight over scarce resources. Earth wails over humanity's wrongs.

As mentioned earlier, to deny science, more specifically, climate science, is to deny truth and the Jesus of truth. Thankfully, many "Creation-care" Christians do appreciate the facts surrounding climate change and are working diligently, hand in hand with science, to reverse the trend.[1] They see Jesus as the firstborn of all Creation and would never intentionally diminish his Lordship by misusing the great gift he made and commissioned us to steward.

When Jesus tells us to pray that God's good governing comes to Earth, he has in mind an Earth that "gives us this day our sustaining bread" (Matt 6:11, translation mine). Yet, Jesus expects us to eschew American greed and live as if "life does not consist in the abundance of possessions" (Luke 12:13–21). Rather than building bigger barns or renting more storage units, we need to develop an ecospirituality that takes every opportunity to recycle resources, reduce pollution, and rejuvenate the Planet.[2] Jesus demands we learn to live with less and work diligently to influence laws and policies that save our fragile Earth.

An initial resource for Christians is the Green Bible which contains well-chosen essays on Creation-care by leading religious scholars.[3] It includes a Bible study guide, a resource guide, an action guide, a list of organizations and web-sites, and a subject index—all with an ecological bent. It highlights in green lettering the biblical passages related to caring for Earth. Thus, a fervent Red Letter Christian is also a committed Green Letter Christian. Also beneficial is a study of The Earth Charter, one of the more significant moral documents addressing global sustainability (can

---

1. Google "Young Evangelicals for Climate Change."
2. See Miller, *Jesus Goes to Washington*, 7–23 for a discussion of "ecospirituality."
3. *The Green Bible*, 17–114.

be googled and downloaded). Then Christians must evangelize to save an Earth, hell-bent.

Those Christians who have boarded the ecological bullet train of "Creation-care," remain faithful to the biblical mandate that Earth belongs to the Lord (1 Cor 10:26 with Ps 24:1). They apply the theology of "preservation" not only to Scripture and the human soul, but also to the Planet (Rom 8:22–23). Out of love for God and others, especially future generations, they have seen the importance of sustainability as an essential part of their faith, their eschatology, and their growing spirituality. In fact, green-conscious spirituality may be the most compelling religious movement of the twenty-first century.

Churches ought to begin assessing the impact of their sanctuaries upon Nature's Sanctuary and make at least minor changes like more efficient lighting, weather stripping, and recycling. Some might consider more significant alternatives such as installing solar panels. The designs of newly built religious structures (and all new construction) should incorporate standard green building principles. Congregational leaders will encourage their people to be more ecofriendly in their homes and businesses, while prodding them to advocate for sustainability at the local, national, and international levels.

Hopefully, all of us lax Christians will repent from our ho-hum attitude toward Earth' woes, come to our senses, and enter the spring of a greener character formation as part of our gospel-worthy walk. It bears repeating that following in Jesus' footsteps now compels smaller and less invasive footprints—ones that trod the path of sustainability. The future viability of this beautiful world, one that declares the glory of God at every hand, is at stake. The more Christians retrofit their character with an ecological sensitivity and respect an ever "groaning" Creation that God declares as "very good," the more we exalt the Lord of Creation.

33
The Progressive Jesus

Jesus believes his mission consists in recovering the subsistence values from his traditions that are necessary for Israel's revival/survival, for the fulfilment of its destiny, and for the justice due to oppressed peoples and Planet. Yet, he faces the ever conquering imperial ethic of hierarchy, ethnic superiority, materialism, and violence—the all-pervasive codes of misery. This ethic, as we have argued, bears a family resemblance to present day American Conservatism. Jesus does not ignore this ethic or capitulate to it, but he covertly, and sometimes overtly, besieges it on every hand through his sayings, parables, healings, exorcisms, and speeches. He counters it with the preeminent indestructible value/virtue/principle; i.e., love, but a love steeped in justice and in the political, social, and economic realities for a sustainable future.

I began by unashamedly affirming that Jesus' moral character, grounded in public love and humility, *directly translates into modern day Liberal/Progressive ideals*. Some Christians might object to "labels," although they do not hesitate being called "Christian." However, from Jesus we learn that one's political/moral identity is just as important as one's religious identity. We are not talking about political parties here, but rather a defined set of *political values*. Most Conservatives do not hesitate to brandish their title with upmost pride (Mitt Romney used the term "Conservative" over ninety times in one campaign speech). Why should Christians not hesitate to name their political ethic, and to do so with conviction, fervor, and honor? We all live by a set of values. Naming them expresses our moral character, essential for our sense of identity and dignity. It also allows us to align with others of the same cast in the struggle against named faulty values. That is

PART 2—EXALTING JESUS

why Jesus does not hesitate to use the label "the Kingdom of God" (also used ninety times) with its set of defined values pitted against the hellish values of Caesar's Kingdom or, for that matter, any corporate imperialism (like the "marts" of worker misery, whether "K" or "Wal").

In his last letters from prison, Dietrich Bonhoeffer pleas for a "non-religious interpretation of biblical texts."[1] It may have puzzled him that so many great German theologians capitulated to Nazism. He raises the possibility that their theological language was so esoteric and ingrown that it could not effectively counter the world of Nazi values. To enter any political struggle, including those shaped by the American mind, we must not hesitate to march under a "non-religious" banner that delineates the biblical values and issues at stake. The terms "Liberal" and "Conservative" remain elusive, nuanced, and overlapping. Yet aptly, they each pose a set of defined and embraced ideals.

We reaffirm that Christ-minded Christians will welcome being named Progressive/Liberal when understood in the following ways:

First, Jesus emphasized *compassion*, the type of love that suffers with the downtrodden. Progressives, too, celebrate empathy or compassion that identifies with victims' pain resulting from unjust social and economic structures and policies. That the virtue of compassion belongs to Progressives is confirmed when Conservatives chide Liberals as "bleeding-hearts," even though recently Conservatives speak of a "compassionate Conservatism." Their version; however, thrives on individual responsibility and downplays social victimization, masking the structural causes of human suffering. Progressives call upon the nation and it leaders to be compassionate communities by promoting sustainability rights for the marginalized and guaranteeing them social, economic, ecological, and political justice. This is the thrust of Karen Armstrong's effort for cities to sign on to The Charter for Compassion.[2]

Second, Jesus hailed *egalitarian ideals* in his "love your neighbor as yourself" principle. He continuously railed against the vast differences in wealth, social standing, and political power. He also affirmed affirmative action in his "last/first" and "humble/exalted" reversal notions in which justice must be restored to those injured. Progressives, too, believe in the full range of justice for more equal outcomes; i.e., a justice that actually reduces great social and economic disparities and attempts to right past

1. Bonhoeffer, *Letters*, 198–99.
2. Armstrong, "The Charter."

social wrongs. These contrast with Conservativism that values hierarchy and permits extreme social and economic gaps, to which it blames the poor for falling between the cracks.

Third, Jesus *decried accumulating material goods* and treasures on Earth. Progressives, too, reject self-centered material motives as fundamental to morality. Economic incentives are always tempered by Jesus' incentive to love the other as yourself or Paul's admonition to consider the interests of others. Progressives reject conspicuous consumption and luxurious living, believing that Earth's resources ought to serve the community first and then individual aspirations. Progressives promote material sufficiency and castigate the wasting of our Planet. Conservatives, on the other hand, value the unregulated freedom to accumulate and dispose of property as one sees fit under the rubric of the "profit motive" or the "bottom line," euphemisms for self-interest.

Fourth, as outlined in his Matthew 25 "Judgment of the Nations" speech, Jesus believed in a coming *Good Governing* that provides free food, clean water, shelter, health care, and dignity to prisoners. He preaches "big" government; so big, in fact, that his Kingdom will dwarf the Roman Empire. Progressives, too, believe in the role of government to provide security, to protect fundamental rights, to right previous wrongs, to meet the full range of its citizen's basic needs and protections, and to spread a wide safety net for the most vulnerable. Governing is built upon justice, freedom, and shalom understood in their broadest meaning of "for the common good." Progressives assume the dignity of every person, which guarantees an ever expanding set of civil rights—especially for persecuted minorities. Conservatives berate "big government," since it regulates business, overtaxes the rich, and redistributes wealth. Yet, ultimately the issue is not the size of government, but what is necessary for its compassion and justice to reach all citizens equally.

Fifth, Jesus was devoted to the Land and a *sustainability ethic*, assuming that Earth is the Lord's and that its flow of milk and honey should wisely meet the needs of all alike. Progressives also insist on a sustainable environment. Distressingly, they recognize the overwhelming evidence that future ecocatastrophe looms as a high probability if drastic steps are not immediately taken. Conservatives tend to be somewhat cavalier regarding the environment and, in fact, often dispute the overwhelming scientific evidence regarding human-induced climate change. They see environmental regulations as government's attempt to inhibit the market's free reign over God's Creation.

Sixth, Jesus, the precursor of modern-day Progressivism, spoke of *nations sitting at the same table* and learning about peace and justice on Earth. Progressives consider all human beings as brothers and sisters, citizens of the world community. Out of love for their country, they eschew militarism with its quick trigger finger. They exhaust every possible diplomatic solution to solve global conflicts and always solicit the role of international bodies like the United Nations. This contrasts with Conservatism's strong nationalism and insistence upon America's superiority that should never concede its interests to any other nation or group of nations.

Last, Jesus, in his "you have heard/but I say to you" sayings, proved that he was not tied to literalism, but believed that law and Scripture need *constant revision and reinterpretation* to address present issues. All renderings; however, hang upon loving justice. Progressives oppose a strict "textualism" and "originalism" (limited to the literal writings and mind of the original framers of the Bible or Constitution) since traditions and creeds can become outworn. For the Progressive, law is never static, but living, and ought to be interpreted in light of the underlying values that create it—compassion, equality, inclusiveness, non-materialism, environmental care, and nonviolence. Conservatives tend to read the Bible or the Constitution more literally to reflect an American Character that morally permits the second-class citizenship of women, blacks, Latinos, homosexuals and other minority groups, the accumulation of excessive wealth, aggressive warfare, and Earth's pollution.

The resemblance between Jesus' character and the modern Progressive's character outlined above is striking. This ethic, based upon being our brother and sister's keeper that emerged from peasant sustainability ideals and weaved their way through the Hebrew Scripture, shaped Jesus' heavenly and earthly mind. His to-the-death challenge of Rome's collective egoism also challenges the American mindset and the Conservative ethic constructed from it. As he hoped to right the wrongs of the imperial character, he compels us to right the historical wrongs of the Conservative character. Authentic spirituality is infused with Jesus' Liberal/Progressive character. By living his character, we walk worthy of his good news, and exalt him above the fractured truth of Conservative values that have fed history's wrongdoings.

34
The Character-transforming Jesus

We have now come full circle. We began by looking at the inadequate drawings (often mere doodles) of Jesus. Although conveying elements of truth, these representations, passed off as the whole, distort or obscure the masterpiece in all its beauty and majesty. Lacking the big picture, Jesus is rendered small and trivial, contributing to the collapse of Christian character. We have tried to present a more accurate and compelling depiction of Jesus by presenting a fuller account of his life as a Jewish prophet born into a Galilean peasant class struggling under Rome's misery-ridden occupation. This backdrop provides the needed shadings to better understand and exalt Jesus by our character in order to carry on his mission more effectively.

Let's return to the popular Evangelical expression: "accepting Jesus Christ as our personal Savior." What does this mean today when Christianity has been so distorted and when so many have turned their backs on religion?

First, as Evangelicals have always emphasized, we must acknowledge that we are sinners—shaped and controlled by Big Me values which ultimately bring ruin to us, others, and Earth. We all lend our minds to little empires at home, at work, and at church as imperial values slither in and take hold. Even though Jesus knocks at our heart's door seeking entrance, we resist his call. If and when we come to our senses, we open that door and invite him in as Savior and Lord. However, we must make sure some pseudo-Christ is not knocking to gain entrance, something disguised as an angel of light. We do not want to let in a distorted cheapened Christ—a pick-and-choose Jesus made in the American image, which legitimates our social, economic, and political interests—or even an Antichrist. We want to welcome in a credible Christ, the exalted Jesus of Scripture. We have suggested that the ancient creeds failed to acknowledge, much less celebrate, his life and teachings, permitting a spiritual carte blanche. The result: a gallery of random brush strokes and disfigured pictures.

Second, we must understand what "accepting Jesus" means. In Evangelical terms, accepting Jesus Christ is to accept the mind or character of the compassionate Jesus into our very being *and* into our daily individual, social, economic, political, and ecological activities. Simply put, his character transforms our character. This means accepting *a specific set of priority values and policies that the historical Jesus promoted*, as we have explored in Part 2. The flip side is that in accepting his person we also reject every other competing mindset or way of life. Salvation, then, also includes transformation *from* something. It uncovers and disavows our selfish character and those instilled, cultural values, fruits of the alien powers. Jesus saves us from the Big Me that paralyzes us and inevitably drives us to construct a small Jesus to justify it. A new spirituality is created and confirmed only by its fruit: love, peace, kindness, goodness, etc. (Gal 5:22–23). This is why deliverance is so profound.

If what we have said is true, then by accepting Jesus into our hearts as Savior we accept: the Galilean, the Jewish, the prophet, the divine, the compassionate, the just, the neighbor-serving, the welcoming, the non-materialistic, the forgiving, the truth-seeking, the peace-loving, the union-of-nations, the Creation-care, and yes, the Progressive Jesus, *and nothing less*. These are the traits that build Christian character. They exalt Jesus, the one who forgives us our sins, especially those imperial-based Conservative sins that plague us all.

In accepting the exalted Jesus as Savior, we affirm him as our Lord and act that out in our daily walk. Possessing the same mind/character as Jesus raises us above the American rat race to engage in a world we are destined to serve. Christians, like Jesus, will act in the political arena and inject a prophetic critique against all political parties, politicians, and policies driven by Conservative/imperial values. That we possess Christ's moral character is confirmed when we: count minorities as equals and treat them with dignity; bridge the vast economic gaps; love Earth through reducing our carbon footprint; and eliminate all the faces of violence so that no bruised woman or beaten child lay hidden behind closed doors and no bullet ridden bodies liter our streets, schools, and battlefields. Christians

The Character-transforming Jesus

will vigorously support Progressive minded candidates and policies, while aware that everyone and everything is subject to sin's corruption. For this reason Christians must always "come to our senses," as Jesus called it when referring to the prodigal son, and walk away from our cultural self-oriented character and back to Christ's other-directed character. It's a journey; however, that never ends.

As a word of final warning, the Christian's involvement in politics must never slide into promoting some religious-specific doctrine. The Progressive values Jesus promoted are universal, which secular-minded citizens can also embrace. Jesus did not create these values during his stay on Earth, but brought them from eternity and dug deep, reinforcing them as he discovered them embedded in the long-standing peasant ethic and Jewish traditions. He became a powerful advocate for them in creative, nuanced, and imaginative ways. For example, even though "Love your enemies" was not forthrightly formulated in the ancient world, the idea is found in the Torah (Exod 23:4–5; Luke 6:27). Out of our love for Jesus and our desire to emulate and please him, we are motivated to live by the universal values (justice, freedom, and well-being) for which he died. Beliefs and doctrines that are specific to a religion have no place in shaping public policy. In this sense, the separation of church and state must always remain intact.

Christians not only *believe* in the gospel and *act* it out, we also *proclaim* it. A magnified Jesus brings good news to everyone, whether justification to the repentant sinner, vindication to the victimized, chastening to the stone–hearted, or change to fossilized structures. We proclaim his *whole* gospel when our minds are set upon his Progressive values. We are to proclaim this good news of Christ's love to every person and nation, yet always remembering the old cliché—we must walk the talk.

We must be ever vigilant because cultural values can easily slip into our proclamation and scandalize Jesus. By embracing and proclaiming imperial/Conservative/American values, Christians bring bad news, not good news, to Earth and to its inhabitants. Thank God, because of Jesus' servant obedience even unto death, we are saved from ourselves and the selfishness that drives our daily lives and our institutions. The powers of darkness could never extinguish such a Great Light. Now, because the "spirit of holiness" (Rom 1:3) is implanted within our character through faith, we are empowered to proclaim Jesus' Progressive values and exalt his name above any other. Now many will bow, confess his Lordship, and adopt his world-changing character.

35
Conclusion

We have questioned some commonly championed, but distorted pictures of Jesus that render him quite small. In belittling him, we make God, his Father, small as well. The blemish that J. B. Phillips so passionately hoped to heal still festers. The Garden of Eden story teaches a profound, enduring, but sad truth that ambition, avarice, and anger are part of our DNA. Our character is so deeply flawed that we even learn how to transform this unholy trinity, normally considered deadly vices, into virtues. Reinforced by our cultural mindset, we spin Jesus to reflect our iniquities, even if unconsciously. Our salvation means a never-ending struggle against our fallen character and culture and a continuing need for repentance, forgiveness, deliverance, and character transformation.

The picture of Jesus we have painted, while always incomplete, attempts to render him a masterpiece for character formation, needed at this time when character does not seem to count for many Christians. We have shown that Jesus reached down to the lowest human level to model the highest divine values by living an inspired and Godly life in humble obedience to his Father. He taught us that humanity is not consigned to the most despicable evils, to moral ignorance, and to human and Earth misery. He wanted to show us "the way" to truth and life through love. His way or path is a spiritual path, but one that winds through everyday life with all its personal, social, economic, political, and ecological stepping stones, as well as its stumbling blocks. Like all the classical prophets, he wanted to save the nation by restoring the neglected moral character of God (justice, freedom, and shalom). He models for us the true empathetic God in whose image we are created. We reflect Jesus and God's image only when we, too,

Conclusion

are compassionate lovers of justice, freedom, and the welfare of all alike and are willing to suffer for these as Jesus did.

For Paul, the Christ-like walk means that whatever we do will be done for the *glory* of God and not for our own vainglory (Phil 2:11; 1 Cor 10:31). The Bible speaks of filling Earth with God's glory as waters cover the sea (Hab 2:14). The seas actually overflow when a Jesus Christ-like love humbly considers others better than ourselves. We can never fully appreciate how profoundly Jesus flooded our world with his self-sacrificing love. It remains the high-water mark of future ages in the face of imperialism's arrogance, greed, violence, false piety, and fraud. Jesus expects us to rise to his sacred mission.

Hopefully, we have been faithful to the spirit of J. B. Phillips who desperately wanted us to worship a highly exalted God of sublime grandeur revealed through Jesus Christ. In his classic book he comments, "We can never have too big a conception of God."[1] The same holds true of Jesus. Even though Christians yearn to magnify him, he is always infinitely bigger than any of our efforts. Yet, every act of self-sacrificing love exalts him before others. We must, then, never give up our feeble attempts to ennoble him and always guard against our continual temptations to degrade him, looking forward to his "well done, good and faithful servant" (Matt 25:21).

Phillips hoped that we would catch "a glimpse of the true God." I pray this work has helped you capture a peek into the life of a credible Jesus. Our deep love for him motivates us to overcome all the tempting distortions, allowing us to build upon his character and walk in its strength. Then our voice becomes his voice and our hands his hands. In summary and conclusion: *our lives become worthy of the Gospel of Jesus Christ when we possess his humble moral character that infiltrates our hearts and shatters the prevailing American Character and makes possible world transformation for God's glory*. What could be better news for our ailing Planet?

We end this work with Paul's final summary exhortation to the Philippians. We must "think about" and "keep on doing" everything "excellent"; i.e., whatever is "true," "honorable," "just," "pure," "pleasing," and "commendable" (Phil 4:8–9). Possessing these character traits, among the others we have championed, form the excellent life worthy of Christ and remains our

---

1. Phillips, *Your God Is too Small*, 120.

immediate and long-term goals. While Paul admits that even he will never fully attain the goal, he exhorts us Christians to always "press on" (Phil 3:12–14). And so, the last words in emulating Christ's character and living his gospel can only be—press on.

Bibliography

Achenbauch, Joel. "The Age of Disbelief: The War on Science." *National Geographic*, March 2015, 30–47.
Alcorn, Randy. "Bummed Out." *The Santa Barbara Daily Sound*, June 2, 2011, editorial.
Alexander, Eben. *Proof of Heaven: A Neurosurgeon's Journey into the Afterlife*. New York: Simon & Schuster, 2012.
Armstrong, Karen. "The Charter for Compassion." www.charterforcompassion.org.
Aslan, Reza. *Zealot: The Life and Times of Jesus of Nazareth*. New York: Random House, 2013.
Bailey, Sarah Pulliam. "White Evangelicals Voted Overwhelmingly for Donald Trump, Exit Polls Show." *The Washington Post*. https://www.washingtonpost.com/news/acts-of-faith/wp/2016/11/09/exit-polls-show-white-evangelicals-voted-overwhelmingly-for-donald-trump/?utm_term=.79114d7b51e1.
Becker, Ernest. *Escape from Evil*. New York: Free Press, 1975.
Bell, Rob. *Love Wins: A Book about Heaven and Hell and the Fate of Every Person Who Ever Lived*. New York: HarperCollins, 2012.
Bonhoeffer, Dietrich. *The Cost of Discipleship*. Translated by R. H. Fuller. New York: Macmillan, 1963.
———. *Letters and Papers from Prison*. Edited by Eberhard Bethge. Translated by Reginald H. Fuller. 2nd ed. New York: Macmillan, 1966.
Borg, Marcus, and N. T. Wright. *The Meaning of Jesus: Two Visions*. San Francisco: HarperSanFrancisco, 2000.
Boswell, John. *Christianity, Social Tolerance, and Homosexuality*. Chicago: University of Chicago Press, 1980.
———. *Same-sex Unions in Pre-modern Europe*. New York: Villard, 1994.
Branson-Potts, Hailey, et al. "Ocampo 'wasn't done with the killings.'" *Los Angeles Times*, January 18, 2012, A1, 8.
Brooks, David. *The Road to Character*. New York: Random House, 2015.
Bultmann, Rudolf. *Jesus and the Word*. New York: Scribner, 1958.
Cadge, Wendy. "Saying Your Prayers, Constructing Your Religions: Medical Studies of Intercessory Prayer." *Journal of Religion* 89 (2009) 299–327.
Calnewsroom. www.calnewsroom.com/2015/03/03/california-ballot-initiative-propose-bullets-to-the-head-for-gays-lesbians/
Campolo, Tony. *Red Letter Christians: A Citizen's Guide to Faith and Politics*. Ventura, CA: Regal, 2008.

Bibliography

The Center on Philanthropy. "Patterns of Household Charitable Giving by Income Group." https:lupui.edu/files/research/giving_focus_on_meeting_the_needs_of_the_poor_July_2007.Pd

The Charter for Compassion. www.charterforcompassion.org.

Conwell, Russell. *Acres of Diamonds*. Uhrichsville, OH: Barbour, 2003.

Dobson, James C. *The New Dare to Discipline*. Carol Stream, IL: Tyndale House, 2014.

Fergusson, D. M., and M. T. Lynskey. "Physical Punishment/maltreatment during Childhood and Adjustment in Young Adulthood." *Child Abuse and Neglect* 7 (1997) 617–30.

Fowler, James W. *Stages of Faith: The Psychology of Human Development and the Quest for Meaning*. New York: Harper & Row, 1981.

Francis, Pope. *Laudato Si': On Care for our Common Home*. Huntington, IN: Our Sunday Visitor, 2015. Gallop Poll. www.gallup.com/poll/155003/hold-creationist-view-human-origin.aspx.

Gershoff, E. T. "Spanking and Child Development." *Child Development Perspectives*, Sept. 1, 2003, 133–37.

Gewirth, Alan. *Human Rights: Essays on the Justification and Applications*. Chicago: University of Chicago Press, 1982.

The Green Bible. The Revised Standard Version of the Bible. Division of Christian Education of the National Council of Churches in Christ of the USA. New York: HarperOne, 2008.

Gushee, David P. "Reconciling Evangelical Christianity with Our Sexual Minorities: Reframing the Biblical Discussion." *Journal of the Society of Christian Ethics* 35 (2015) 141–58.

Henry, Carl F. H. *The Confessions of a Conservative: An Autobiography*. Waco, TX: Word, 1986.

Jeremias, Joachim. *Jesus' Promise to the Nations*. Translated by S. H. Hooke. Studies in Biblical Theology 24. London: SCM, 1958.

Kant, Immanuel. "On a Supposed Right to Lie from Benevolent Motives." In *The Critique of Practical Reason and Other Writings in Moral Philosophy*, edited and translated by Lewis Beck, 346–50. Chicago: University of Chicago Press, 1949.

Käsemann, Ernst. *New Testament Questions of Today*. Translated by W. J. Montague. New Testament Library. London: SCM, 1969.

Keener, Craig S. *The Historical Jesus of the Gospels*. Grand Rapids: Eerdmans, 2009.

Kelsey, George. *Racism and the Christian Understanding of Man*. New York: Scribner, 1965.

Klein, Naomi. *This Changes Everything: Capitalism vs. the Climate*. New York: Simon & Schuster, 2014.

Kohlberg, Lawrence. "Moral Stages and Moralization." In *Moral Development and Behavior*, edited by Thomas Lickona, 31–53. New York: Holt, Rinehart & Winston, 1976.

Krasner, Barbara and Boszormenyi-Nagy, Ivan. *Between Given and Take: A Clinical Guide to Contextual Therapy*. New York: Brunner/Mazel, 1986.

Lakoff, George. *Moral Politics: How Liberals and Conservatives Think*. Chicago: University of Chicago Press, 2002.

Mead, Margaret. *Blackberry Winter: My Earlier Years*. New York: Pocket Books, 1975.

Meier, John P. *A Marginal Jew: Rethinking the Historical Jesus*. Vol. 4, *Law and Love*. New York: Yale University Press, 2009.

Miller, Douglas. *Jesus Goes to Washington: His Progressive Politics for a Sustainable Future.* Eugene, OR: Wipf & Stock, 2013.

Molineaux, Alan. "Could Your Evangelical Church Be Called a Cult?" http://www.redletterchristian.org/evangelical-church-called-a-cult/ (April 23, 2014).

National Urban League's. *The State of Black America.* 38th ed. 2014. http://nul.iamempowered/com/content/national-urban-league-launches-38th-edition-state-of-black-america.

O'Reilly, Bill. *Cultural Warrior.* New York: Broadway, 2006.

Patterson, James, and Peter Kim. *The Day America Told the Truth: What People Really Believe about Everything that Really Matters.* New York: Prentice Hall, 1991.

Phillips, J. B. *Your God Is Too Small.* New York: Macmillan, 1961.

Phillips, Kevin. *American Theocracy: The Peril and Politics of Radical Religion, Oil, and Borrowed Money in the 21st Century.* New York: Viking, 2006.

Putnam, Robert D., and David E. Campbell. *American Grace: How Religion Divides and Unites Us.* New York: Simon & Schuster, 2010.

Rand, Ayn. *The Virtue of Selfishness: A New Concept of Egoism.* New York: Signet, 1964.

Reimers, David M. *White Protestantism and the Negro.* New York: Oxford University Press, 1965.

Robinson, Marilynne. "A Proof, a Test, an Instruction." *The Nation,* January 2/9, 2017, (special edition) 16–20.

Samarin, William. *Tongues of Men and Angels: The Religious Language of Pentecostalism.* New York: Macmillan, 1972.

Scott, James C. *The Moral Economy of the Peasant: Rebellion and Subsistence in Southeast Asia.* New Haven: Yale University Press, 1976.

Stearns, Richard. *The Hole in Our Gospel: The Answer that Changed My Life and Might Just Change the World.* Nashville: Nelson, 2009.

Surowiecki, James. "Why the Rich Get so Much Richer." *The New York Review of Books,* September 24, 2015, 34.

Weber, Max. *The Protestant Ethic and the Spirit of Capitalism.* Translated by Talcott Parsons. New York: Scribner, 1958.

White, Lynn. "The Historical Roots of Our Ecological Crisis." *Science* 155 (1967) 1203–7.

Wright, N. T. *Jesus and the Victory of God.* Christian Origins and the Question of God 2. Minneapolis: Fortress, 1996.

Zabloski, Jim. *The 25 Most Common Problems in Business and How Jesus Would Solve Them.* Nashville: Broadman & Holman, 1996.

DOUGLAS J. MILLER graduated from Wheaton College, Fuller Theological Seminary, and Claremont Graduate School. He was Professor of Christian Social Ethics at Eastern Baptist Seminary (now Palmer Seminary) in Philadelphia, Pennsylvania. He pastored the First Baptist Church of Santa Barbara, California, and is the author of *Jesus Goes to Washington: His Progressive Politics for a Sustainable Future*. His work appears in *Christianity Today*, *The American Baptist Journal*, *Baker's Dictionary of Christian Ethics*, and *The Evangelical Dictionary of Theology*. He passed away on May 2, 2017.

www.ingramcontent.com/pod-product-compliance
Lightning Source LLC
Chambersburg PA
CBHW031433150426
43191CB00006B/499